PRAISE FOR
BOLD AS LOVE

"*Bold as Love* is a moving expression of Bob Roberts's life's work in breaking down barriers and promoting greater understanding and reconciliation among Christians, Muslims, and Jews."

— Jimmy Carter, 39th
President of the United
States and founder of the
Carter Center

"In Bob's new book, *Bold as Love*, he lays out a masterful practical guide on a revolution of love taught by Jesus of Nazareth. Loving like Jesus transcends all cultures and religions. Bob proves by his experience that it works. It is a must read."

— David M. Beasley, former
governor of South
Carolina

"What an inspiring, practical, life-changing book! Bob Roberts shows Christians how to stop being awkward around those of other faiths and instead engage in respectful, honest, and authentic friendships. This book challenges what we may believe about others as well as what we think we know about ourselves."

— Dale Hanson Bourke,
author of *Embracing Your
Second Calling*

D1304454

"Bob Roberts is willing to take hits to do what God has commanded us to do: Love those *not* like us. Read and digest this book. It's from a front-line practitioner who is crazy about Jesus and all the people of the world."

— Dave Gibbons, founder of
Newsong, HopeMob.org,
and Xealots.org

"This is a book bouncing with energy and brimming with hope—with wise truths jumping off every page. Bob Roberts shows how you can have deep differences with people and also deep love for them, how you can fundamentally disagree with their faith while finding great beauty in it, and that learning about another tradition only helps you grow in your own."

— Eboo Patel, president
and founder of Interfaith
Youth Core and author of
Sacred Ground

"In *Bold as Love* Bob Roberts invites us to join him on a journey of courageously loving people no matter what their belief, nationality, or religion. Bob is a world traveler and a brilliant student of culture and I can think of no one better to write such a book. If you are daring enough to learn how to love people different from you, read *Bold as Love*."

— Dave Ferguson, lead pastor
of Community Christian
Church and lead visionary
of NewThing

"*Bold as Love* is not only for evangelical Christians but for Muslims, Jews and people of faith (and also none) interested in the whole arena of multi-faith engagement—interfaith dialogue with action. Reading this, I felt not only my own faith, resolve and perspective strengthened, but I felt a greater sense of solidarity and contentment, because Bob Roberts was finally articulating all that I had been thinking about."

— Amjad Saleem, the
Cordoba Foundation

"Bob Roberts pioneers a way for us to engage the increasingly multi-faith, multi-cultural context we call earth. But this is no mere theory for Bob. In *Bold as Love* this wonderful, brave, courageous, winsome Texan actually shows us the way by putting his life on the line for the Gospel. Go Bob!"

— Alan Hirsch, author of
The Forgotten Ways and
The Permanent Revolution

"You have done what each one of the great spiritual masters like Zarathustra, Confucius, Moses, Krishna, Buddha, Jesus, Muhammad, Nanak, Baha'ullah and other great masters have done, that is doing your share in building a cohesive America, where no one has to live in apprehension, discomfort, or fear of the other."

— Mike Gouse, president
of America Together
Foundation

"*Bold as Love* is a true contribution to multi-religious dialog and understanding. Bob Roberts is a bold man who represents who Jesus is. I embrace his urgent wisdom of moving from fear to love."

— Tom Dine, senior policy advisor, Israel Policy Forum; former executive director for AIPEC

"Bob Roberts is a rare and unique modern missionary. Remaining deeply rooted in his Christian faith, God has given him the gift of engaging people from all over the world. His is a ministry of love and respect. *Bold as Love* is his Second Half story."

— Bob Buford, author of *Halftime* and *Finishing Well*

BOLD

as

LOVE

BOLD

as

LOVE

*What can happen when we see
people the way God does*

BY BOB ROBERTS, JR.

THOMAS NELSON
Since 1798

NASHVILLE DALLAS MEXICO CITY RIO DE JANEIRO

Published in Nashville, Tennessee, by Thomas Nelson. Thomas Nelson is a registered trademark of Thomas Nelson, Inc.

Published in association with the literary and marketing agency of C. Grant & Company, Wheaton, Illinois.

Thomas Nelson, Inc., titles may be purchased in bulk for educational, business, fund-raising, or sales promotional use. For information, please e-mail SpecialMarkets@ThomasNelson.com.

Unless otherwise noted, scripture quotations are taken from THE ENGLISH STANDARD VERSION. © 2001 by Crossway Bibles, a division of Good News Publishers.

Library of Congress Cataloging-in-Publication Data

Roberts, Bob, 1958—
    Bold as love : what can happen when we see people the way
God does / by Bob Roberts.
        p. cm.
    Includes bibliographical references.
    ISBN 978-1-4002-0420-5
    1. Christian life. 2. Globalization—Religious aspects—
Christianity. 3. Evangelistic work. 4. Roberts, Bob, 1958– I. Title.
BV4501.3.R6256 2012
248.4—dc23   2012025339
Printed in the United States of America

12 13 14 15 16 QG 6 5 4 3 2 1

To Prince Turki al-Faisal of Saudi Arabia: You represent your faith and your part of the world in an exceptional way. With love, respect, and admiration. I will always be grateful for our friendship. You have made me a far better Christian by causing me to think deeply about what I believe and challenging me to reach over to those who believe differently than me, not just around the world, but right in my home of Fort Worth–Dallas, Texas.

To my close Jewish, Muslim, Christian, and secular friends in the Nyon Process, all twenty-eight of you. To my Muslim friends in particular, this book contains all I have told you both publicly and privately; the message is the same. I love you all deeply and pray for you regularly, as some of you do for me.

Finally, to my Imam Zia at the Irving Islamic Center. I love you with the love of Jesus and I know you love me as well. You have been a friend and have experienced as an imam much of what I have as a pastor in this regard.

CONTENTS

ONE

BOLDLY LOVING ALL MY NEIGHBORS

And behold, a lawyer stood up to put him to the test, saying, "Teacher, what shall I do to inherit eternal life?" He said to him, "What is written in the Law? How do you read it?" And he answered, "You shall love the Lord your God with all your heart and with all your soul and with all your strength and with all your mind, and your neighbor as yourself." And he said to him, "You have answered correctly; do this, and you will live." But he, desiring to justify himself, said to Jesus, "And who is my neighbor?"

—Luke 10:25–29

Nikki, my wife, and I drove all over Dallas–Fort Worth looking for kosher or halal meat. We barely knew what it was and didn't have a clue what made it different, but we had to have it, and time was running out.

We were desperate. An imam and a rabbi, along with their congregations, would be coming to our worship services the next morning, and the imam and the rabbi were coming to our home for lunch. This would be like no Sunday lunch I had ever experienced either as a boy growing up in a pastor's home, or as a fifty-year-old pastor of a megachurch. Nikki had researched online to make sure everything was prepared properly according to Jewish and Muslim tradition, but the meat was a problem.

Finally, we found a grocery store in north Dallas with a roast—the only one left and the only piece of kosher or halal meat in the entire store. At this point, we didn't care if it was a good one or a bad cut of meat, we just needed something. Roast it was, and roast it would be for lunch. We were as excited as two kids unwrapping presents at Christmas.

This Sunday occasion had come about not because I had some grand plan of getting to know Jews and Muslims, hoping to bring our congregations together. It was an unexpected series of events in which relationships morphed into friendships. I had been taught to believe that these were people merely to convert; friendship was a luxury I didn't think I had time for. But this luxury turned out to be not only vital and most exciting, but an experience that deepened my love of Christ and others in ways I could never imagine.

Starting the Journey

This particular event was birthed when I was challenged by an unlikely and unexpected friend from the Middle East. I was visiting Prince Turki al-Faisal, a humanitarian, statesman, and the founder of Saudi Arabia's modern intelligence service. He is the son of former King Faisal of Saudi Arabia and the grandson of King Abdul Aziz, the founder of the current Saudi monarchy, established in 1902. It goes without saying that he is also a Muslim.

I had first met him a few months earlier at a dinner in Lisbon, Portugal, where we both served on a think tank established by the United Nations under the Alliance of Civilizations. Called the Nyon Process, it was a handful of people gathering to talk about how to bridge the gap between people and religions (more on this dinner later). As a result, he later invited me to visit Saudi Arabia so we could get to know each other better and discuss ways to bring greater understanding between Christians and Muslims.

And I did.

At one point during the dinner in Lisbon, Portugal, the prince asked me, "What about Dallas, your home city—what are you doing there?"

I told him, "Your Highness, do you realize how hard it would be to do something between Muslims and Christians in Dallas, the buckle on the Bible belt? I don't mind being innovative, but I'm not suicidal! My Baptist and evangelical brethren would skin me alive for that!"

My friend responded, "All the more reason you should do it there. If you can do it there, you can do it anywhere. Dallas should lead the way."

I have to give it to him: he really knew how to motivate a Texan. We like to do the impossible.

A New Texas and a New World

Prince Turki may have had an intuition about Dallas that I didn't have at the time: how utterly diverse it had become in my lifetime.

The most diversity I experienced growing up was knowing a Catholic. That was about as wild as it got in Lindale, Texas, with a population of 1,043. Yes, there were African Americans in deep East Texas, lots of them, but they belonged; they had been there a long time, even if my subculture didn't always treat them right. But who were these Catholics? At the time, there wasn't even a Catholic church in Lindale. Catholics had to drive to Tyler to find a Catholic church.

There was a day when faith was tribal and defined by geography. Not anymore. Every religion is everywhere. Even in Dallas. Today, 44 percent of the population were not born in an English-speaking nation; 238 languages are spoken in the DFW area; 28 percent of the population don't speak English in their homes! We have Little Pakistan, Koreatown, Little Iran, Little India, Little Arabia, Chinatown, three Little Vietnams, four Little Mexicos, Little Nepal, Ethiopia/Eritrea.

Hispanics make up a large portion of the metroplex with roughly a million people. But there are also 40,000 Arabs, 90,000 Chinese, 25,000 Colombians, 5,000 Egyptians, 80,000 El Salvadorans, 7,500 Cambodians, 8,000 Bangledeshis, 15,000 Ethiopians, 90,000 Indians, 40,000 Iranians, 20,000 Ismaaelis, 50,000 Koreans, 25,000 Nepalese, 25,000 Nigerians, 10,000 North Africans, 50,000 Pakistanis, 30,000 Filipinos, 40,000 Polish, 22,000 Puerto Ricans, 80,000 Vietnamese, and dozens of other ethnicities. If this is Dallas—the jewel of Texas in the churchgoin' God-fearin' South—what about where you live?

In 1975 there was one mosque in the entire DFW

area. Today there are forty-three. The closest mosque to me is about two miles away, the closest Buddhist temple is four miles, and the closest synagogue is five miles. The whole world is around me—and it's around you. What an opportunity! What a time to be alive!

But let's face it, we've got mixed feelings about this new world. We've all had that feeling when we find out the person who moves next door to us is a Muslim. We feel it when a gay couple holding hands in the mall wearing matching pink T-shirts that say "Jesus loves me too!" catches the attention of our small children, and we have to explain in a way that holds on to who we are but makes clear who they are but in a loving way. God has allowed us to be born and be alive at a time when we will run into all sorts of people who need to know the love of Jesus.

What's happening in the DFW metroplex is happening in many other cities in America and in the world. Two books that look at how immigration is changing our world are Doug Saunders's *Arrival City: How the Largest Migration in History Is Reshaping Our World,* and *Exceptional People: How Migration Shaped Our World and Will Define Our Future* by Ian Goldin, Geoffrey Cameron, and Meera Balarajan.

Others are noting how other forces of globalization are shrinking the world and making Everyplace a global reality. Note especially Fareed Zakaria's *The*

Post-American World (Release 2.0), Niall Ferguson's *Civilization: The West and the Rest*, Jeffrey Sachs's *The Price of Civilization: Reawakening American Virtue and Prosperity*, and Thomas Friedman's *That Used to Be Us: How America Fell Behind in the World It Invented and How We Can Come Back*. In their book *God Is Back: How the Global Revival of Faith is Changing the World*, John Micklethwait and Adrian Wooldridge, editors at the *Economist*, also note how all religions are growing globally, and what impact that is going to have.

So we are doing a good job at seeing what globalization means for economics, education, engineering, science, and communications—although especially as it relates to religion, it's leaving some people mystified and others afraid.

I sat on a plane with an executive from Ernst & Young, a Fortune 100 company. This executive had just heard several global speakers talk about many such troubling future trends. He was really shaken up about the implications for America and his children. He said the only hope was for people across the world to connect with one another in a meaningful way, or it would be decades of war between the haves and the have-nots.

He asked what I did, and I told him I was a pastor. That's when he said earnestly, "What are you doing to prepare the church for this? It's serious, man."

It is serious, but from a gospel perspective, it is also one of the greatest opportunities in history. I meet born-again Christians in the Middle East and Muslims in the West and New Agers everywhere. Now the conversation is between orthodox Christians and Jews, Muslims, Hindus, Buddhists—you name it. There is no privacy anymore—everything is in the global public square. We have to learn to speak with one conversation and give the same message everywhere to everyone.

In the past, we would have one conversation with ourselves, one with our family, one with our tribe, and one with the world. Each conversation was suited to the audience. How do we speak in a globalized world with everyone listening? More importantly, how is it heard by people not in our tribe? There are multiple faiths all around vying for converts, promising salvation, and claiming to be the way.

It is both an opportunity and a nightmare. It's an opportunity for us to share and live out our faith as "missionaries" at home, but a nightmare if we disrespect cultures or don't realize the power of what our words can do. Islamophobia is no joke in the West, and recently in the news from Egypt they were talking about "Christianophobia." How do we respond? What are we to believe? What is the truth? I've discovered we often don't really speak *to* others; we speak *about* others to our tribe, promoting the way our tribe perceives things. It's time for us to learn to communicate a clear and consistent message. When the world hears us, and they google us, if the language isn't consistent, it creates serious questions.

Everything is everywhere like never before in the history of humanity. The world is changing at a rapid pace, and with it your neighborhood, school, work, mall, and everywhere you go. For the first time in history, the whole world is showing up everywhere and changing the neighborhood.

Nothing is more critical than how civil society is being shaped before our very eyes. In the past it was missionaries or diplomats who brought information back from the other side of the world and told us how to interpret it, but not anymore. With the whole world present everywhere, a traditional understanding of communication of faith and of foreign policy is shifting. Diplomats refer to track-one and track-two diplomacy. Track one is diplomat to diplomat or government to government. Track two was popularized by Eisenhower, which is people to people. More is being shaped by track-two diplomacy than track-one. The Arab Spring is a living example of how people are bypassing governments to communicate with one another and establish new norms of behavior in civil society. Though I don't foresee the overthrow of our nation, I do see shifts as we come to know folks from all over the world who are moving in next door to us.

In the past we had track-one religious leaders inter-preting what to say and representing us in what was said. Now we are thrust into the middle of relationships with people from other parts of the world, and we have to fig-ure them out without benefit of a neighborhood religious leader. Furthermore, what a religious leader identifies as important and what an everyday follower of a religion sees as important are not always the same thing. How do we relate to this new reality?

Are We Ready?

I believe these immigrants hold the keys to our future. Their presence in our neighborhoods enable us to connect with the rest of the world economically and culturally. They can serve as significant bridges and opportunities for Americans with the rest of the world in business, edu-cation, and every domain of society. When we love people and build relationships with them, all kinds of good things happen that were not previously possible. I think this is a partial answer to the businessman who was so worried about the future.

More centrally for Christians, in a very real and literal way, we get to be missionaries—to tell people from all over the world about Jesus. And that can have a multiplying effect. Have you ever thought about how effective it would be if immigrants led to Jesus in our neighborhoods were to reach back to their friends and family in their native lands? The opportunity for non-Anglo-Americans to spread the gospel globally is unprecedented.

But I sometimes wonder if we're ready. In June 2011, the Pew Research Center released the results of a survey called "Global Survey of Evangelical Protestant Leaders."[1] They interviewed evangelical leaders who gathered at the Lausanne Committee for World Evangelization. The results give a glimpse into the challenges facing the world church when it comes to reaching out to other cultures and religions.

First, we learn that in places where there is no persecution of Christians—as in the Global North—only 44 percent said they believed the church is stronger than ever; 54 percent said it's the same or worse. But in the Global South, where persecution of Christians can be very severe, 71 percent said the church is stronger than ever—and they were optimistic about the future!

It's also interesting how these Christian leaders viewed other religions: 65 percent had negative views of Buddhists and Hindus, 67 percent had negative views of Muslims, and 70 percent had negative views of atheists; Jews were viewed negatively by only 25 percent. The question, of course, is: How can we view *any* religion or people group negatively when we've been called to love them all and share the good news of Jesus with them?

Our negative feelings are often matched by insensitive actions. As noted above, many of us are in the habit of speaking *about* others, rather than *to* them or *with* them. We know how to speak our tribal language, but not how to speak to other tribes. Neither do we realize sometimes how we are coming across. When I visit Christian websites that attempt to evangelize other groups, I try to imagine myself as one of the people they want to reach. I often find I'd be offended by their stereotyping and condescending attitude.

Another model is offered by Paul in Colossians 4:3–6:

At the same time, pray also for us, that God may open to us a door for the word, to declare the mystery of Christ, on account of which I am in prison—that I may make it clear, which is how I ought to speak. Walk in wisdom toward outsiders, making the best use of the time. Let your speech always be gracious, seasoned with salt, so that you may know how you ought to answer each person.

Look at the words he uses: *clear, wisdom toward outsiders, making the best of time, gracious* speech, *know how you ought to answer.* In other words, sharing the gospel is more than giving the Romans Road plan of salvation or the four Spiritual Laws. It's not me giving a set of facts for others to act on, but listening to them, understanding where they are in their lives and faith, and dealing with their questions—all the while sharing how Jesus makes all things new.

It's not going to be easy learning a new way of relating to people of other faiths, but we have one of the most effective multifaith evangelistic manuals ever created. It's called the Bible.

A New Testament Era Today!

The Bible is nothing if not a book about migration, globalization, different faiths mingling and mixing—and Jesus Christ speaking to it all.

Every great move of God has always involved migration: Noah; Abraham the pilgrim in the Holy Land; Joseph in Egypt; from Egypt to Canaan with Moses and Joshua; David to Jerusalem; and Jesus and his call for the gospel to be taken to the ends of the earth. This is how the sovereign God spread his word all through ancient history—and how he's doing it now.

Note especially how our situation today is so much like that in Paul's day. Look at Paul at Mars Hill (Acts 17). In his sermon, he began by meeting people where they were, even complimenting them, before moving forward. But much more is going on here than an example of how to speak.

In his article "One World, Under God," in the *Atlantic*, April 2009, Robert Wright set Paul's ministry to other faiths in its historical context:

> The origins of Paul's doctrine of interethnic love . . . emerges from the interplay between Paul's driving ambitions and his social environment. . . . In the Roman Empire; the century after the Crucifixion was a time of dislocation. People streamed into cities from farms and small towns, encountered alien cultures and peoples, and often faced this flux without the support of kin.

Wright goes on to note how this situation is like the turn of the twentieth century in the United States, when industrialization drew Americans into turbulent cities, away from their extended families, and into "families" like Knights of Columbus and Rotary Club. He continues:

> Indeed, Roman cities saw a growth in voluntary associations. Some were vocational guilds, some more like clubs, and some were religious cults (*cults* in the ancient sense of "groups devoted to the worship of

one or more gods," not in the modern sense of "wacky fringe groups"). But whatever their form, they often amounted to what one scholar has called "fictive families" for people whose real families were off in some distant village or town.

The world we minister to is very much like the world Paul ministered to. The point is, we needn't scratch our heads and wonder what in the world we're going to do in this new world. God has given us not only the strength of his Holy Spirit but the wisdom to be found in the Scriptures. The message of the New Testament and the example of the church's first missionaries (especially Paul) can be so helpful for us today.

A Time for Bold Love

The late Jimmy Hendrix used to sing a song titled "Bold as Love." Love is bold. Think about your first love, your first kiss, your first boyfriend or girlfriend. It was a risk to reach out. Would you be rejected and brokenhearted? Or would there be reciprocation? Probably a little of both! We believers in Jesus are commanded to take the good news of Jesus to every single person on the globe. We are commanded to love God and love others. And sometimes that requires risky boldness.

We can only love those we know personally. Furthermore, we cannot practice this bold love of people unless we first focus on God. I reach out to someone I don't even know, not because I love that person—I probably don't, because I don't even know him or her—but because my bold love is directed at Jesus and following his commands to love others. I express bold love toward others because he first expressed bold love toward me. I am responding to his bold love.

We live in a day when we must be bold as love and take the first step as followers of Jesus. It was radical when Billy Graham went to Russia to preach; he was criticized for meeting with "godless atheists." We must be equally radical in our day. But we don't need to go to Russia, China, or Saudi Arabia; we need only look around at our workplaces, in our neighborhoods, and in our cities to see people from all over the world. God has brought the world to our nation. What a gift! He's calling all of us to love. We all get to be missionaries of love on our streets and in our neighborhoods.

End of the Story

Let me get back to the story I started this chapter with, to show how it came together for Northwood Church.

As I returned from the Nyon Meeting in Lisbon with

Prince Turki al-Faisal, I realized that though I knew a handful of Muslims in the United States, I didn't know a single Muslim in the Dallas–Forth Worth area. As I flew in and out of DFW airport, I had often wondered about a large mosque with a green roof I could see from my plane window. But that was about it. So when I returned to Dallas after my visit with Prince Turki, I was determined to change that.

I contacted a Muslim American friend in Washington DC, Suhail Khan, who connected me with Imam Zia of the Irving Islamic Center, the mosque I see as I fly over Dallas, and a young Egyptian Muslim businessman in the DFW area, who in turn introduced me to Rabbi Jeremy Schneider of Temple Shalom in north Dallas.

I set up a meeting with Rabbi Schneider and Imam Zia, and we met on the Wednesday before Thanksgiving in 2009. We actually met at my church—which, looking back on it, was probably a hard thing for Imam Zia to do. One lesson I've learned is that when you reach out to someone, you approach him on his turf; asking him to yours makes him defensive from the very beginning.

At first Zia was skeptical. You have to understand, this is Dallas and I'm a part of the big Baptist tribe—not a tribe that has been the most hospitable to Muslims in the United States. It's not unusual to hear leaders from my tribe on national and local news accuse the prophet

Mohammed of being a pedophile or Islam of being a demonic religion.

Rabbi Schneider was also very skeptical and curious why I would want to meet with him, let alone a Muslim. He was used to evangelicals who supported Israel for their own theological reasons, without really supporting the Jewish people.

I told both of them about the many friendships I have all over the world, and that some of my Muslim friends had challenged me to do something in Dallas to connect Christians, Muslims, and people of other faiths. I made it clear that I was an evangelical, a conservative Christian, and that I didn't like interfaith gatherings: I saw interfaith as loosey-goosey, let's all just hug one another and ignore core truth. I wanted nothing to do with that. I liked the concept of *multifaith* better, which says we have fundamental differences, but the best of our faiths teach us we should get along. I wanted to do all I could to build relationships, so instead of living in fear, we could live in peace with one another.

I don't know if they believed me; I'm sure they wanted to believe me, but this was a stretch. I was a Texas evangelical megachurch pastor of the tribe of Baptist reaching out to the "opposition." My tribe had caused both groups more grief than any other group. Could they trust me? Would they have a mess to pick up with their own people if things didn't work out? They took a huge gamble on me, but I was the only one who had asked them to dance, so I offered my hand, they took it, and I will forever be grateful. This was bold love for them and for me—but it would build a bond of friendship that continues deeply to this day. I also told them I didn't want us to get into theology (we all disagree around the person of Jesus); we should be clear there is no hidden agenda. Instead we should build friendships before we start talking God and religion. They agreed. So at the event, I stated that Jews see Jesus as one of many would-be messiahs, Muslims see him as a prophet, and we Christians see him as God. But we can and should still be friends.

The imam and the rabbi liked this approach, so we decided we would embark on a journey: we would combine our congregations for a weekend event that coming January.

We began on Friday night with all three congregations going to the synagogue to have kosher desserts and to participate in a Jewish worship service. That was followed by a question-and-answer time with the imam, the rabbi, and myself. The next day we repeated the process at the mosque. Sunday everyone came to our church. We three Dallas clerics were excited, and a few people in each of our congregations participated, but most were scratching their heads a little. (Actually they were scratching their heads a lot!)

We had a few interesting moments during the event, to be sure. When our three congregations met at the synagogue, a Jewish woman (formerly a Southern Baptist) asked me, in a somewhat accusatory manner, if I really believed Jesus was the only way. I told her, "Ma'am, I really do. I don't say that in an arrogant way or a condemning way—just a New Testament way, like Jesus said himself. Let me also say, this is a multifaith event. We aren't going to condemn one another for what we each believe, but we want to be honest about what we do believe. How can we have a true relationship if we don't know what each other truly believes?"

Imam Zia came to my rescue, saying, "Ma'am, because Bob has not accepted the Prophet Mohammed as from God, he is in trouble according to my tradition." I was grateful; it was his way of saying, "We're all going to hell!" We just need to learn to be nice the way we say it. That was the spirit that we tried to model during the whole weekend.

I can't tell you it went without a hitch. In my congregation, several members were really upset we had invited Muslims to our church. They didn't mind inviting Jews; Muslims, for some reason, were another story.

This reaction stunned me, because since 1995 our church had been working intensively with people in

Vietnam. Hundreds of our members have traveled to Vietnam and worked with the government there to serve the poor. We've been connecting members in face-to-face projects. Nearly a hundred exchange students have come to live with our members in the DFW area to go to local universities. We have Vietnamese leaders, diplomats, and businessmen in our church all the time. We had learned to love the very place where so many Americans had died, ruled by a government that was officially communist.

I thought working with Muslims in our own community would be easy. I was wrong. Those who were most upset would no doubt fund missionaries to go witness to Muslims overseas, but they wanted to isolate themselves from Muslims who lived in our city—and in many cases lived in our neighborhoods, attended our schools, and shopped at the same stores we did. Unfortunately, a small group ended up leaving the church over this issue.

So I was especially grateful for those from our church who did attend the event. Some had questions, but they came wanting to love others unconditionally. I had been engaging people from all over the world for some time, telling my congregation stories of meeting Muslims, Jews, communists, and others who had become friends—and our people loved it. Now instead of hearing stories, they were becoming part of a story. For many of them, taking the risk to love their neighbors was as radical and bold for them as it was for me to be in Afghanistan, Gaza, or some other war-torn place in the world.

By the end of the weekend, people were deeply appreciative. One said to me, "I didn't understand what difference it made whether or not I engaged others near me—I do now." Another added, "Why haven't I seen this before? These people want to be our friends. How can they hear the good news of Jesus if we don't even love them and befriend them?"

Getting to Know You

I watch politicians and diplomats, and I admit that they frustrate me sometimes. They have conferences, seminars, think tanks, and talk-a-thons on how we need to get along and what public policies need to change. But I don't know of a single conference that has ever accomplished that. They may provide policy papers (which hardly anyone reads, understands, or executes). Instead, love in action moves the ball forward, and does so like nothing else. It connects people, and that's what can begin to make a difference. We are all stuck in the mud. Diplomats don't understand faith in the world, and religious leaders don't understand the world—but that is a luxury we can no longer afford.

Having a big event that the clerics could pull together was fine, but I've discovered we need far more than that if we are going to connect and get along. It has led to several smaller initiatives and things people have done on their own to connect. There are so many non-threatening things that can be done to allow us to get to know one another. From that first gathering, several women came together and formed a cooking club. It was composed of eight Christians, eight Jews, and eight Muslims. One Monday night, Nikki warned me within an inch of life to be sure and *not* stop by the house, because at these meetings the Muslim women remove their *hijab*s—and no men are allowed to see them without their *hijab*s. They call their group "Embrace." They take turns cooking at a Christian's house, a Jew's house, and a Muslim's house. They talk about their food, culture, and stories.

I once tweeted about my wife's warning, and Imam Zia tweeted back, "Welcome to my world, Bob!"

At one meeting, Nikki explained to them the Christmas story, and why it matters to Christians. She told them about the incarnation and the grace that came as a result of it. That led to a lot of questions and answers. The following month, they went to the mosque, where Imam Zia explained Islam to the group.

Zia and I have become good friends. A few months

ago he wanted to go hunting. This is Texas, and we all love hunting and our guns. He was born in Pakistan and raised in England. I told him, "Zia, I'm from East Texas; if you show up hunting in your Pakistani garb, and I give you a 12-gauge, and we go running through those woods yelling *Allahu akbar*, we're gonna die. I'll take you, but I want you in jeans, a T-shirt, and talking with a Texas accent."

We had to get up really early to get to the lease (the land we leased to hunt on) as the sun came up. As we approached the property, Zia asked me, "Bob, can I stop and pray?" The thought of being on a country road in the Texas woods with an imam stretched out on the ground made me a little nervous, but I told him, "You bet."

We pulled over, he faced Mecca, and began to pray. I took a knee and prayed to Jesus with all my heart. Someone in a loud pickup truck passed. At first I kept one eye open, in case of some trouble. Then I thought, *Oh well, he'll just think we're a couple of Jesus freaks.* We finally got out to the lease and walked and gave turkey calls. At first we were going to hunt wild boar—but pork doesn't go over too well with Muslims. As we began to give the turkey calls, we heard one and we began to move toward it; we had a male call and we could hear the female calling back. We kept our guns ready and couldn't wait to see that female turkey coming toward us. All of a sudden the bushes began to rustle, and we couldn't wait for the turkey to emerge. But it wasn't a turkey—it was a man with a female turkey caller. We could have wound up shooting each other!

I think that's often how we are when engaging with people of other faiths. We hear someone else, we begin to move toward him, and, if we aren't careful, we shoot him before we even have a chance to begin a relationship, let alone a conversation. Sadly, we didn't shoot any turkey that day, but we did go fishing briefly in a fishing hole, and Imam Zia caught a fish. The morning was well spent just hanging out—Muslim and Christian clerics along with an MD who took us hunting.

We are now planning an outing in which we will take ten imams and ten pastors from Dallas and hang out for three days in the woods to hunt, fish, and just get to know each other. There are challenges—like getting *halal* food—but it's worth it. Some of the group have never shot a gun before and worry that they'll get in trouble.

As a boy raised a Southern Baptist, I was in the organization called Royal Ambassadors, the missions education arm for Southern Baptist boys. I memorized this pledge:

As a Royal Ambassador I will do my best: to become a well-informed, responsible follower of Christ; to have a Christlike concern for all people; to learn how to carry the message of Christ around the world; to work with others in sharing Christ; and to keep myself clean and healthy in mind and body.

I grew up believing that, and I still do. I sometimes quote it in addresses I give to pastors. I've never forgotten it.

Loving others isn't something we do when we agree with them, or when they're like us, or even when we like them. Loving others was made for when it's hard, scary, and near impossible. Our faith wasn't made to live in a vacuum or isolation. It's something we do face-to-face, heart-to-heart, hand-to-hand. I like to tell our members that we are to love to the extreme. If Jesus really is the way, the truth, and the life, then I must love in extremes, with respect and kindness, or others may never get to hear this gospel that is found only through Jesus.

Multiple faiths are all around vying for converts, promising salvation, and claiming to be the way. It can be seen as a nightmare—or an opportunity for us to share and live out our faith as missionaries at home.

This book is about what our congregation has experienced while becoming missionaries in a multifaith world, and how it has deepened our love for Jesus and enhanced our witness for him. Read on if you want to find out how you can join us in what we believe is a new movement of God in this changing world. It will require boldness.

I have a young pastor friend, Micah Fries, who pastors the Frederick Boulevard Baptist Church in St. Joseph, Missouri. He holds a conference called 1:21; the concept is to take the mission and theology of the first-century church and apply it in the twenty-first century. Sadly, we often do eighteenth-century missions for a twenty-first-century world. It's time we catch up in a bold way that loves others boldly.

TWO

CONFRONTING ALL MY FEARS

Be of good courage, and let us be courageous for our people, and for the cities of our God.

—2 Samuel 10:12

He who dwells in the shelter of the Most High will abide in the shadow of the Almighty.

—Psalm 91:1

This multifaith journey can be a little intimidating—if not downright frightening—at times. Take my first trip to Gaza. There I was, in the summer of 2009, at the border between Israel and Gaza. I was with a friend from another country who had many friends in Gaza, so we were somewhat secure in going there. My friend wanted to see if I could help facilitate the access of medical professionals to the area.

At the time, I had watched on television the bombardment of Gaza by the Israelis and listened to all the reports on CNN. Two deadly foes were in a deadlock of violence. Hamas was interviewed. On the news I watched an Israeli helicopter scope out a vehicle, then blow it up. *This is a bad place to be,* I thought. *Am I an idiot? These Palestinians and Jews have never been able to get along. I'm no diplomat.*

Having worked in war-torn countries elsewhere, I'd learned that everything isn't as black-and-white as what I am often told back home. There is good and bad mixed together with every situation. I've also learned that some of the greatest things in my life come from frightening times of obedience. Bold love has its cost, but it also has its own unique reward.

When we love boldly, God's presence is bold upon us in those situations. So I serve as a follower of Jesus, and the people I meet often ask me questions. I tell them the Jesus stories in our New Testament and they tell me stories from their Quran. I honestly feel God's presence at these times, stronger than nearly any other time in my life. Sometimes people in the West wonder why we see so few miracles, why we see God do so little; I believe it's because our faith and love is shy and unengaging—our culture doesn't demand radical love and obedience and yet those are the only things that God works in response to.

In Gaza, I was taken to meet a couple of dozen various community, business, and government leaders. My friend introduced me as "a Baptist evangelical pastor from Texas." Not the way you really want to be introduced to a group our government calls terrorists! Was he trying to get me killed?

All kidding aside, I was nervous. And irrational thoughts crossed my mind: *What if they take me as a hostage? What if I can't escape? What should I do? How do I handle this?*

Five Fears to Overcome

When we think about reaching out to people of other faiths, there are at least five fears we're confronted with.

We have to deal with these fears because we've been called to be salt and light in the world, not isolated from everyone else and disconnected. It's time for us to learn to live our faith in public. To do that, we must overcome our fears.

1. Physical harm.

I wasn't seriously concerned about my physical safety the first time I went to Gaza, but the second time I visited, I was.

A few months later I returned to Gaza with the friend who took me there the first time. But at the last minute, he couldn't go, so I had to proceed by myself. I was a little nervous, but I'd done this before and knew the drill. Besides, my Gaza friend would be waiting for me on the other side.

Going through the border security process is a little unnerving on both the Israeli and Palestinian sides. From the Israeli side, you go through a series of compartments, where you put your bags, clothing, and the like in bins and wait as you move from one compartment to the next. Even though the building is empty—there aren't many people going into Gaza from Israel—it can still take several hours to cross. You don't see anyone; they talk to you from speakers and tell you what to do next. In rooms above the terminal, you see soldiers and others looking down on you, watching as you go through the screening.

Then begins a long walk through some pastures and a farm in a kind of demilitarized zone. The walk is maybe a half-mile, and you can see about a half-mile to the right and left. As you walk, you see a few bombed-out buildings, craters from bombs, destroyed vehicles, scorched earth. Behind you the Israelis are watching closely; in front of you, the Gazans are also watching closely. There are young boys shepherding sheep on both sides of the walk. I wonder why in God's name they would be there—but it's the only place they can graze their animals. Automatic, camera-sensitive unmanned machine guns look down on everyone—Jesus help me walk inside the lines!

Carrying my bags, I finally got to the other side, where my friend was supposed to be waiting for me. But he wasn't. A cab pulled up and the driver told me that my Gazan friend was held up at a meeting and that I was supposed to come with him. I didn't know what to do. The situation didn't feel right. It could be dangerous. This man could be here to kidnap me. Immediately in my heart I began to pray. I could either turn back and return to Israel, or I could take this man at his word and get in the cab with someone I didn't know.

I've come to understand what Paul meant when he said "pray without ceasing." I was praying fast and in the moment, if not with my eyes closed. In that instant of wide-awake prayer, I sensed God saying, "Go. I'm with you." So I took a deep breath, got in the cab, and put my trust in Jesus for whatever would happen. I was glad many minutes later when the cab driver pulled up to my Gaza friend's office—I was safe! Relatively speaking . . .

In America, the physical dangers aren't great at all, but we've seen so many movies depicting angry Muslim terrorists that it is sometimes hard not to be afraid of Muslims. We know it's not fair or kind, but when we see a Muslim board our plane, the thought of hijacking crosses our minds. So we know physical fear at some level even in the States. When we began to have Muslims come to our church, many of our members were fearful that we would be blown up. Some left, most stayed, and all received according to what they sowed. Those who sowed fear still live in fear and want others to live in fear. Those who sowed bold love have built friendships and serve as bridges for others to cross over.

2. Hostility from "enemies."

We had a big event at our church in 2010 called the Global Faith Forum during which evangelicals and people of other religions came together and spoke of faith and how it impacted everyday life. They were from all over the world and included leading businessmen, royalty, world leaders and diplomats, imams, priests, rabbis, pastors—you name it. A young married Muslim couple, originally from the Middle East, wanted to get some books on the Trinity and Christianity. I took them to a Christian bookstore—and when we got there, I wished I hadn't. Right beside all the theology books were books that dealt with the second coming of Christ, and most were very negative toward Muslims and people in the Middle East, using language that was frankly hostile and unloving. Unfortunately, it's the type of hostility Muslims sometimes expect from us, and it's not unlike the hostility we sometimes expect from Muslims.

When I met Prince Turki at that dinner a few years ago, the organizer of the dinner introduced me to him as "an evangelical pastor from Texas." Immediately, in front of everyone in the room, Prince Turki looked at me and asked, "Why do you evangelicals all think we in Saudi Arabia are the antichrist?"

I asked him why he would think that. Apparently the Saudis are well aware of what is said in this country on some religious television shows and in some religious books. I had to give him and everybody there a crash course on dispensational premillennialism; I pointed out that not all conservative Christians agree with its interpretations of the Bible!

Afterward, I wondered if the producers of those Christian television shows realize what kind of message they are sending around the world. They beam material into the Middle East exalting the Jews while trashing Islam and Muslims. Do they realize how hostile it all comes across?

In Gaza I was actually more concerned about hatred of me, as an American and as a Christian. We've all seen the angry demonstrations in the Middle East on CNN, and we assume this represents how all Muslims feel about us. It is the same situation as our evangelical television shows in reverse. It's no wonder that when we get into a room with each other, we expect hostility.

The Lord has gifted me with a strange sense of humor, and sometimes it comes in handy. It has shown me that sometimes humor can defuse a tense and potentially hostile situation. So when it was time for me to speak with those Gaza leaders, I figured I'd just plunge directly into talking about evangelicals, since my friend had introduced me like that. I asked them, "How many of you have heard of an evangelical?" They all raised their hands.

"How many of you know an evangelical?" I continued. No one raised a hand.

"How many of you have a negative view of evangelicals?" They all raised their hands. I was nervous.

I said, "Well, contrary to what you all may have heard—we are not all terrorists!"

They laughed. This broke the ice, so they began to

ask me questions, and we had a good, friendly conversation after that. But one reason the humor worked was because all of us had experienced the atmosphere of hostility, sometimes through the media and sometimes in our own personal encounters with people of other faiths.

3. Hostility from "friends."

I mentioned in the last chapter that a few people left our church when we held a multifaith event there. I've also received angry e-mails from fellow Dallas Christians because of our multifaith work. This disappoints me, but no longer surprises me. When we first get involved in this type of work, we are afraid—and for good reason sometimes—of what our brothers and sisters in Christ will think of us and say to us.

Sometimes people ask me, "Aren't you afraid of being used by others?" My response is always the same: "I can't help how people may use it, but I want to make sure I give them an accurate representation of who Jesus is. They are my focus when I'm with them—not my tribe." Jesus went to the heart of his opposition—and it wasn't from the "other" tribe, it was from his own.

I learned many years ago that when you love boldly the religious establishment gets very nervous. There are categories of people without Jesus we love to hate and fear, and categories of people who don't know Jesus whom we want to reach. Jesus has only one category—he loves all people and wants them to come to know him.

The early church first feared Paul because he had been a persecutor of the church. They wouldn't accept him. Then they feared him because he opened the doors of the church wide open to include Gentiles. If Paul were here today, I have no doubt with whom he would spend his time.

4. Losing one's faith.

Some Christians hesitate to get involved with people of other faiths because they are afraid they are going to lose or compromise their own faith in the process.

For example, some people think because of this ministry, I've become a liberal or mainline Christian. Not at all. I'm an evangelical, a conservative evangelical at that, and an evangelistic evangelical to top it all off. This means I tell everyone I can, in a polite way, about Jesus. I believe Jesus really is the only way to God. But that doesn't mean I'm better than anyone else or that this gives me a right to be arrogant. Truth is wrapped in boldness, but with humility, not arrogance or hate. No, I still believe in the Great Commission, that everyone should get to see and hear the gospel at work so they can make their own call about Jesus. I just happen to think multifaith is the best way to do that!

I've also discovered that building relationships with people of other faiths has helped my faith become stronger. I've known Prince Turki for five years now. No one has challenged me more or made me think more about my faith. Recently, on my trip to Saudi Arabia, a reporter for the *Arab News* came to interview us at the King Faisal Center for Research and Islamic Studies. During the course of the interview, I told the reporter, "You know, Islam has made me a much better Christian."

"What?" the man asked, looking surprised.

I said, "Yes. First, you were the people I feared the most. So when I began to love you, I had to love you as my 'enemy,' because the Bible says we should love our enemies. But I found out you weren't my enemy. You forced me to love to the extreme, which is what Jesus requires. Second, you also made me think deeply about what I believe and why I believe it, so I went deeper into my own faith."

5. Fear itself.

In the midst of the Great Depression, Franklin Delano Roosevelt famously said, "We have nothing to fear but fear itself." It's true. We know fear breeds a great deal more fear, and it's not that easy to deal with sometimes.

I had heard of the tunnels that link Gaza and Egypt, so I talked my host into taking me to see them. They're huge, truly a massive network. There are more than twelve hundred tunnels. Until the recent Arab Spring, when the border with Egypt and Gaza was opened, this was the only way to get fuel, food, and other supplies into Gaza so people could just survive. These are not tourist sites, for sure, and there is a lot of danger involved in using them, from collapse to explosions.

Over each tunnel entrance was a tent. We would go inside the tent, stand on a small platform above the shaft with three or four others and be slowly lowered thirty feet or so. When we hit the ground, we had to bend over; the tunnels weren't made for tall or big people, and the walls were very narrow and uneven. Some were shored up with boards; others with just sand. It was very sandy; I could understand how they would collapse easily. I could hear a generator humming that was supplying electricity to the simple lights strung on the ceiling of the tunnel. We walked far enough in so that my friend's cell phone—still working underground!—picked up Egyptian wireless service. At that point he said we should go back.

I thought to myself: *Here is a city of 1.5 million people caged up and without access to supplies—except through these dangerous tunnels. How could anything good come out of this? Keeping people confined like this only breeds the next generation of terrorists.*

When we emerged from the tunnel, we got in our vehicles, and as we were leaving, we saw all kinds of activity, with flashing lights, ambulances, and a curious crowd gathered outside one of the tents. We went over to see what was going on. We were told that a group of young men had gone to Egypt to buy gasoline, and as they were returning through the tunnel, something sparked and ignited the gasoline, creating an explosion.

Another young man was preparing to go in. I assumed he was an expert in getting people out of the tunnels, but he wasn't; he was a relative of the five teenage boys inside. The next day I heard six boys had died in that tunnel, and I couldn't help but wonder if that young man was the sixth.

And I realized that this entire situation was created by fear—Israeli fear of Palestinians, and Palestinian fear of Israelis. Fear building on fear, until it created this seemingly hopeless, inhumane situation.

This type of fear easily crosses borders. We live in a world in which the media is everywhere, from national and international news to blogs and Twitter. What we do in one place affects another place. So when I threaten to burn a Quran here, someone else on the far side of the globe will want to burn Bibles, or worse, kill Christians—which is exactly what happened when the Florida pastor threatened to burn the Quran. When we fight a mosque being built, we are just making it harder for Christian churches to be built in other lands where people may be fearful of Christians.

Looking to God's Promises

These fears are real for everyone, and I have experienced all of them, at different times with different levels of strength.

One reason I was able to move forward in Gaza in spite of being afraid was two verses from the Bible. No two verses mean more to me in all the world than the two I quoted at the beginning of the chapter. And they each have a personal history with me.

The verse from Second Samuel came alive for me when I was in Vietnam. Our church was praying about working there, about what to do and whether to focus on Hanoi. I was sitting in a Vietnamese church in 1995 when I read that verse in my daily Bible reading. For a Christian church to try to work openly in Vietnam would have been thought impossible at the time. Naturally, when I read 2 Samuel 10:12, "Be of good courage, and let us be courageous for our people, and for the cities of our God," it encouraged me and the church to move forward in what seemed an impossible venture.

Psalm 91 became especially meaningful to me when

I was on my way to Afghanistan for the first time. At the time, a full-fledged war was going on. I felt both anticipation and fear, even though I knew I was supposed to go there. But obedience to Jesus in my life had always been tied to holiness or doing something spiritual for God; it had never been a matter of life and death.

In the midst of my anxiety, I read this:

He will cover you with his pinions, and under his wings you will find refuge; his faithfulness is a shield and buckler. You will not fear the terror of the night, nor the arrow that flies by day, nor the pestilence that stalks in darkness, nor the destruction that wastes at noonday. A thousand may fall at your side, ten thousand at your right hand, but it will not come near you. (Psalm 91:4–7)

When I read that psalm on my way to Afghanistan, I believe God was telling me to move forward; through the psalm he was saying, "I'm with you." I don't think he was necessarily promising that he was going to preserve my physical life—I think it's possible to move forward in God and still lose your life. But once I received this promise, I was able to proceed with confidence.

If we think about it, we'll realize that we have no reason to fear, because no one can hurt us—we go to heaven when we die. As Jesus said, "And do not fear those who kill the body but cannot kill the soul. Rather fear him who can destroy both soul and body in hell" (Matthew 10:28).

Recall the story of John Wesley, when he was on a ship returning to England after having served a parish in Savannah, Georgia. He had yet to come to a warm, personal, trusting relationship with Christ, and when the ship encountered a horrible storm, Wesley panicked. But he noticed that the Moravians on board were as calm as if it were a sunny day. One of the Moravians, seeing Wesley's fear, asked him, "Aren't you a believer? Then why are you so afraid?" That's what led him to reexamine his relationship with God, eventually leading to his true conversion to Christ.

But I have great news—most of us are never going to be put in a position of extreme danger for our faith. And as we begin to love those of other religions and cultures, we can depend on the promises of God. Only the promises of God, and the power that comes from him, can enable us to reach out to those who may intimidate us.

From Fear to Love

As God's promises have helped me move forward in multi-faith encounters, I've discovered an amazing thing: the people I fear the most invariably become the people I love the most.

Take the Vietnamese. I was afraid of the Vietnamese, and of communists in general, because of the horrible things portrayed in the media about the Vietnam War. But as I came to know the Vietnamese, I have come to love and care about them. Yes, in conversations with them, I find my beliefs challenged sometimes; the Vietnamese have helped me think more philosophically. Though I continue to disagree with them on various issues, I count some of them as my best friends. As I write this, for example, I received a Christmas and New Year's card from the Vietnamese ambassador to the United States, whom I now consider a good friend.

Or take my relationship with Muslims. After 9/11, I thought, *Thank you, Lord: I work with those red communists instead of those angry Muslims!* Of course, I had no inkling that I would eventually be involved with Muslims or Afghans. But God has a sense of humor. I've come to love Muslims deeply and enjoy hanging out with them. Muslims have also forced me to think deeply about what I believe theologically and why I believe it. My wife is a close friend to many Muslim women in the DFW area and around the world.

What we will come to see as we move from fear to love is this: there is no reason to fear others, because most people *want* a relationship with us.

Take, for instance, my first trip to Gaza. I stayed in

the home of an influential man and his family. We shared a meal together. I discovered that he loves God—not like I do, but in his own way. His devotion is deep. He was educated in the United States. His kids love him. When we arrived at his house, his wife and daughter embraced him. His children played with him. His daughter is in high school, a little younger than my daughter. His son is the age of my son, and he's just gotten married.

The family told me the fear they felt being confined to their home with shelling going on around them earlier in the year. In a different time and circumstance, this man and I could be best friends. He told me his story, and I told him mine, especially of my getting to know Muslims in Afghanistan (more on this later). He was intrigued that I was an evangelical and had so many Muslim friends. I'm not sure he knew what to make of it at first.

We sat up late, and he told me stories from the Quran, and I told him stories from the New Testament about Jesus. He had many of his friends come over, and we all shared our views of God.

The point is that this man was as interested in getting to know me as I was in getting to know him. I have found this to be true time and again as I've met people all over the world—especially when I get to know people who are supposed to be my enemies.

We must simply realize that some of the very people we tend to be afraid of are actually trying to reach out to us sometimes. Recently I was in a meeting with an imam who serves in Memphis, Tennessee. He was born and bred in Houston, Texas, and earned a PhD from Yale University. He is of Indian decent.

When he assumed responsibilities at the mosque in Memphis, he said he felt a little isolated. He wanted to connect with Christians in that part of the country, but they wouldn't meet with him or have anything to do with him. Yes, in a single week, he was invited to church six times, but when people found out he was a Muslim, and an imam at that, they backed away.

Knowing I am from a Southern Baptist background, he asked me if I could help. I asked him if he'd tried to visit with some of the Southern Baptist pastors there. He's been rebuffed a couple of times, unfortunately. But recently I've found some young pastors who are excited about meeting him.

Fear steadily rises to reinforce negative stereotypes and doesn't stay static. But Jesus had an answer for that: He said, "Love your enemies." Jesus was brilliant when he said this, because it is impossible to love someone and still be his or her enemy. In other words, as Christians we have no enemies.

I do not believe all Muslims are terrorists, although

it's clear that a small minority are. But I cannot allow my fear of a small few to paint an entire people in a negative way. I wouldn't want others to paint all Christians a particular way based on a few nutcases. Even so, we mustn't forget God loves even the most extreme sinners. He sometimes turns persecutors into top leaders in the church. Remember Paul?

One thing we can do to love people of other faiths is to clear up their misconceptions about Christians when we have the chance. And when we're in conversation with them, we'll have that opportunity.

Remember Prince Turki's comments about Christians thinking Muslims were the antichrist? In my discussion of dispensationalism, I told him that not all evangelicals believe the temple in Jerusalem has to be rebuilt or the Jews must all live in the Holy Land in order for Jesus to return. I told him in the Old Testament the temple represented God's presence with his people, and was the place where sacrifices were performed for the forgiveness of sins. But because Jesus came, he put his temple in our hearts, and now we don't go through a priest but straight to God. The prince was shocked, because he thought all evangelicals believed the temple had to be rebuilt.

When I was in Doha, at the World Islamic Forum, I spoke at a workshop. Once again, I was introduced as an evangelical, so I explained what that meant. As usual, most people there thought that meant I loved Jews and hated Arabs. I told them I loved Muslims and Arabs, too, and that I equally supported Israelis *and* Palestinians. They were so excited, you would have thought I'd said I was going to become a Muslim.

But there is nothing like spending lots of time with a person of another faith to break down the misunderstandings and the fears. Prince Turki and I have spent a lot of time together, in the United States and in Saudi Arabia. Just recently, my wife, my daughter, and I returned from spending a week with Prince Turki and many in the royal family. The highlight of the trip was going out with him and most of his family. His wife and daughter are great. His young sons are a blast. There is a warmth and calm in the family.

Prince Turki arranged it so I could meet with various people, including twenty-five top leaders in the country. We talked about doing people exchanges, where Saudis could come to the United States for two weeks, and Americans could go to Saudi Arabia for two weeks— exchanges between imams and pastors, women, young people, business professionals, whomever.

I get so tired of people saying the world is closed. People are ready to connect! And once you break through those barriers of fear, wonderful things start happening.

Stepping Out in Faith

This doesn't mean it's always easy. There will be times when we will feel deeply afraid or unsure. We can't necessarily wait around for a happy feeling before we move forward. After all, following God sometimes entails sacrifice and taking up one's cross.

There is no such thing as safely following God.

Isn't it interesting how "unchristian" Christians act when faced with a crisis? It's the end of the world, so hoard food and supplies and buy guns and hide out and wait. That's crazy. When we do things like that we are resisting God and what he is doing. We are also eliminating ourselves from being part of what God is doing.

Our current way of relating to the world is not just un-Christlike and bad for our faith; it's unsustainable globally and sets us up for conflict and war. It's bad for the world. Often in the States we fail to realize that our attitudes and views create an atmosphere that promotes, endorses, and even sometimes encourages war. When we try to figure out exactly when Jesus is coming back, who is good and who is bad, who we can trust and who we can't, then we wind up acting like the rest of the world and become driven by fear, which leads to violence.

If we are going to follow Jesus, we will have to do it in a global way. It's our world. A CEO of a major corporation recently said the new local is global; there is no such thing as simply local anymore. For the Christian this really isn't new; it's the way God has always worked. He's a global God who made the world global and started a global church in Antioch. We are blessed like no other time in history: global is now at our doorstep. But fear will undermine our ability to be a part of the greatest movement of God since the early church!

There is a lot of fear coming and going from every tribe and faith on the planet right now. The only solution is to engage one another. When driven by fear—as followers of Jesus—we cannot love deeply and truly.

We want security; God wants exposure so that he's glorified. We want ready-made plans for every challenge; God requires faith and trust to follow him. We want faith without risk and ministry without pain. But what we'll find is that the most difficult times of life are often the most fruitful times.

The day-to-day reality is this: when we reach out to someone of another faith, chances are nothing bad is going to happen. We have more of a chance of dying in a car than being killed by a terrorist. The media encourages us to blow our fears all out of proportion. But in the end, God is sovereign and in charge of everything; nothing is going to happen without his divine approval and his glory.

Let's turn the tables. What would it be like to be a

Christian in Iraq or Iran or Syria? We would be the minority, and some in the majority wouldn't like our being there. They'd fear we were going to undermine their country and their values. This is a part of everyday life for people in different parts of the world. This is everyday life for Muslims in the United States. When we hear that a mosque or a Buddhist temple is being built in our town, how do we respond? Think about it.

Southern Baptists believe in missions and fund them to the tune of hundreds of millions of dollars, yet in the case of the imam in Memphis, we have a man right in our backyard and yet no one wants a relationship with him. This is shocking and sad. As mentioned earlier, I've found some young pastors who are excited about a relationship and an older pastor who's willing to risk it; but the risk isn't about what the imam will do to him, but what *his own congregation* will do to him.

When the Embrace cooking club started meeting, at first everyone was a little nervous and cautious, because they didn't want to say something wrong. Nor did they want to be put in a position where they'd have to compromise their faith or be viewed negatively. But now Nikki tells me, "We are so beyond just cooking—we've really become friends." Many of the women now connect outside the cooking club.

Nikki recently called me, saying, "A bunch of us are going out together for a girls' night out Friday night; just wanted you to know I won't be around!" It made me glad.

In the end, we have no reason to fear because we've been filled with the Holy Spirit. The Holy Spirit is the comforter and is with us at all times, in all places, in every situation. I can relax and be calm knowing that.

There are so many promises associated with the Holy Spirit. The Holy Spirit will fill us. The Holy Spirit will comfort us. The Holy Spirit will guide us. The Holy Spirit will give us the words we need when we need them. Through the Holy Spirit, God lives in us. And there are dimensions of the Holy Spirit we simply will not experience until we are out on the edge. It isn't us; it's God doing what he wants to do. Jesus said he did only what he saw the Father doing. We do that as well when the Holy Spirit has full reign in us. There is nothing any more indispensible than being filled with the Spirit and walking with the Spirit on a daily and moment-by-moment basis.

Recently, I got a tweet from a young pastor in Washington DC asking me how he should approach getting to know his local imam. He was a little nervous, maybe even afraid. He was led by the Spirit to get started, but he didn't know what to do next. It was all so new to him.

I told him, "Take the imam to a restaurant that has

halal. Then have him over to your house where your families can connect. Then take him waterskiing! God has placed you right where he has because he wants to use you to show the love of Jesus, even if the person doesn't accept who we believe Jesus is. At least it may bring down the tension a little bit, and even make you think about your faith a lot more deeply."

We have nothing to fear but fear itself, and the best way to deal with that is to take some simple steps forward in faith. When we are bold as love, we fear *what we will miss out on* more than we fear what others may do to us. Bold love doesn't ignore the fear; it steps into the place the fear is, and puts its feet squarely on love. That is the place from whence we alone can stand without fear. Who do you fear the most? That person will require bold love of you.

THREE

USING ALL MY FAITH TO GET OUT ON THE EDGE

So everyone who acknowledges me before men, I also will acknowledge before my Father who is in heaven, but whoever denies me before men, I also will deny before my Father who is in heaven.

—Matthew 10:32–33

Our church had a tough year in 2010 for several reasons, but one of the things that made it so was our focus on reaching out to the Abrahamic faiths. People were fine with connecting with Jews, but not with Muslims. As I've mentioned, there was a price to be paid: some members left the church because of our outreach to Muslims. Then again, a number of people joined because of it.

At any rate, in 2011 we thought we'd play it slow and light, catch our collective breath, heal from some of the wounds. I'd come to know Zia over the past two years and would stop by the mosque to see him, and he'd drop by our church. We enjoy hanging out together. That was enough.

Still, for the tenth anniversary of 9/11, he and I thought we might do something more to have our two congregations get together. We decided to invite several imams and other Muslim leaders to a meeting at our church in May, along with Christian pastors and leaders. We had about ten Christians and ten Muslims come to an organizing meeting. We told them we wanted to do something in our city that kept the tension down between our two faiths. Everyone seemed open to the idea.

I wanted to hold the event on the Sunday night of

9/11. But several of the Muslims didn't like that and wanted to do it a week later. They were afraid; the hijackers had been Muslim. Many said they felt like they were apologizing all the time for what "those murderers" and "criminals" (as they called them) had done. They were tired of that. The conversation moved back and forth between having a single event to having a number of events that could build bridges over the long haul.

At our next meeting, held at the Carrolton mosque, everyone was still interested in the 9/11 anniversary event, to be held on September 18. So, we talked excitedly about what it would take to have three or four hundred Muslims and an equal number of Christians show up. At previous smaller events, relatively few people showed much interest, so I didn't have my hopes up.

As the event drew near, we put posters in the seven or eight churches, and ten or so mosques. I invited several local area pastors, but I wasn't convinced that many would come. (I've had calls and private meetings with several pastors who said they really wanted to be involved but were either afraid of the Muslims or of people in their own churches.) I didn't push it too hard at my own church other than a few posters and a couple of announcements. I didn't want our people overwhelming the few Muslims I thought were going to show up.

Then things turned for the worse. A local woman

with the Tea Party started sending letters to her constituents and the press, criticizing what we were doing. She said it was dangerous, that we were being duped by Muslim terrorists who would eventually try to take over the church.

When I first heard about it secondhand, I thought it was a joke, but when I got a call from a local reporter asking me about it, I knew it was no joke. Later it wound up being discussed on the nationally syndicated Mark Davis talk show on KRLD. I was grateful for his response: instead of passing judgment, he said, people should go and just see. I was hoping that would calm things down.

Still I was worried. Worried that only a handful of Muslims and Christians would show up, and worried that the wrong type of Christian or Muslim would. I asked God to protect us, because I was pretty concerned. How could I ever forgive myself if something happened?

On the morning of the event I made an announcement at church by asking the congregation, "How many of you live near a Muslim? How many of you work with a Muslim? How many of you go to school with a Muslim? How many of you have seen a Muslim in the mall? So why not gather with them tonight and build bridges of friendship?"

After the second worship service, I got a call from one of the imams saying he had more than one hundred people coming just from his mosque. Then another called and said the same thing. That was the first indication that something was up.

Multifaith Is Trending

I didn't realize at the time that the idea of Muslims and Christians meeting and working together was trending. Later that month, LifeWay Research reported that in the previous ten years, the number of multifaith gatherings had doubled, from 6.8 percent of churches to 13.9 percent.[1] During that same period, multifaith community service projects nearly tripled, jumping from 7.7 percent to 20.4 percent.

On top of that, people who originally rejected the multifaith interactions were coming around. As previously mentioned, at Northwood we had families leave when we held an Abrahamic Faith Pilgrimage event in January 2010. But less than two years later, at least one family had come back. They said they'd been resentful, at first, of all this talk that to their minds only amounted to "dining with the enemy." But now they were moved to get involved.

Christians especially are discovering that moving from isolation to conversation doesn't mean we have to syncretize our faith or compromise what we believe at all. Truth is not relative. My experience is very common: I have relationships with neighbors and others who are not religious or who come from a different denomination, and I'm able to be their friend without changing my beliefs. People are discovering that it's no different with people who wear a *hijab*.

Some people fear exposing their children to people of different religions. They're afraid they might either become attracted to the other faith, or turn away from God because "no one can agree on religion." That has not been my experience. If anything, it may keep them strong in the faith, especially when they do leave home.

When our children grow up and head off to the university or the workplace, they will meet people from all different walks of life, with different views of God. If you give them that experience in the context of a Christian home and local church while they are still living at home, you'll have the opportunity to answer their questions and give them a good foundation. My son and daughter have been with me all over the world with people of different religions, and it's not only strengthened their faith but helped them learn how to relate to others with more love.

My daughter, Jill, has become close friends with many of the refugees who come to the Dallas–Fort Worth area through World Relief. She even encouraged our youth to get involved with these refugees, and that has gone over big for our teens. For Thanksgiving, our family held a brunch at our house, and then we all headed to an apartment complex where we gave away a turkey to some of her refugee friends.

People are rediscovering that Christianity is a world religion, and has proven itself strong enough to stand on its own feet in the face of other religions. It can take the challenge from atheism, Buddhism, Islam, Judaism, animism, and any other philosophy or religion. The strength of a religion or faith is not what it is when left alone but what it is when it is challenged. Hard times make for strong faith, deep learning, and moving closer to God.

Some are not so concerned about compromising their faith as they are about offending people of another faith. My advice to such people is simple: "Don't worry, you will! And guess what? They won't hold it against you. Guess what else? They'll offend you! But they won't do it deliberately." In other words, Christians are discovering it's not only time but it's okay to embrace people of other faiths in love. More and more people are showing bold love. They are starting with a neighbor, a work associate, a schoolmate, someone at the gym. They are building relationships.

For these and other reasons, more and more Christians are reaching out to Muslims, Jews, and people of other faiths. It's a small movement still, but growing, as I discovered on September 18, 2011.

Overflow!

The gathering at Northwood was scheduled to start at 5:00 p.m. I had sensed that we might have more people than we expected, so I was running around all afternoon, making phone calls to get more food. I had told everyone we'd have *halal* Texas barbeque ribs! The man who was supposed to get us those *halal* ribs couldn't, so we had to scramble with kebabs and other things. Our women's Embrace group was preparing some food as well, but I ordered more, just to be safe. And still I underestimated.

As I was helping set things up forty-five minutes before the service was to begin, a couple of cars packed with Muslim families pulled up. I greeted them, *"Assalamu alaikum,"* which means *peace be upon you*. They responded *"Alaikum salam,"* which means *and upon you, peace*. I told them they'd have to wait in the foyer, as the doors wouldn't be opened for a bit.

Fifteen minutes later, two more vans full of Muslims pulled up. I greeted them, and then went in the auditorium to make sure everything was ready. I met some of the speakers, who'd arrived early, and then went back out in the foyer. The next thing I saw was a big forty-six-passenger bus pull up, packed with people. They began to pour out—men, women, young, old, youth, children!

I grabbed another greeter and staff member to greet them. They were grinning, and so was I. Then another bus pulled up, and another, and another. Then cars started pouring in. I felt like I was at a Billy Graham meeting! The hallways got so packed we had to go ahead and open the doors to let the people in so they could find a place to sit. Ushers were working like crazy getting everyone inside. I had told my people that it's not proper to shake a Muslim lady's hand, but in the confusion some shook hands with women anyhow. (I later told the audience, "Our men were not making passes at your women," and everyone exploded in laughter.)

Ten minutes before we began the place was packed. As I walked in and moved around and shook hands, I was so moved. I began to weep but tried not to let anyone see me. I thanked God in my heart that there were so many Muslims in our church. I was meeting imams and people from all over the world who had moved to Dallas. Had Northwood Church been directed by shy faith instead of bold love—had the people who got upset and left our church determined the direction of outreach for our church—we would never have seen this day. This day was worth whatever price had to be paid. To affirm hundreds of Muslims, to share our faith in a public forum, to serve, love, and connect—it was worth it. It was worth the cross, which had to go through Pharisees and Sadducees; it would be worth the cross weaving its way through "religious" and "Baptist" Christians as well.

Our auditorium holds 2,000, but ended up with 2,500 people that night. There were 700 Christians, and about 1,800 Muslims. I was shocked. I went down to the front row where Zia was. I told him, "Zia, you and I can disagree all we want about God, but one thing I know for sure is this—God is very, very pleased tonight that we are together." Zia grinned and said, "I agree with that, Bob. God is pleased."

I welcomed everyone and introduced myself. The service began with a Muslim man announcing the call to prayer; I wanted our people to hear what it sounded like. We Christians sang the doxology, "Praise God from Whom All Blessings Flow." It wasn't a worship service, but in my heart, I did worship. How could I not? I worship with messed-up evangelicals every week. Worship isn't about who is around me, but to whom I'm directing my attention.

Then a young lady wearing a *hijab* sang "The Star Spangled Banner." The pastors and imams all came forward and we introduced them. Azir Azzez of the North Texas Islamic Association brought a message. Kevin Cox, pastor of Heartland Community Church, said, "Muslims are my neighbors and that is why I'm here." Zia brought words and tried to pronounce his newly learned Texas words. We had a combined children's choir sing "You Are My Sunshine," and I interviewed ladies in the Embrace cooking club.

I said I couldn't speak for all Christians, just for those of us that night. I said, "We love you Muslims with all our hearts. I love Jesus with all my heart. I honestly believe he is God. I know to you that's heresy, but I believe it so much so that I want every one of you to know who he is. So much so that I'm willing to make my own tribe upset with me so you can know a Christian. But as much as I would want you to know him, I would never force you or anyone to be a Christian; it has to be a choice. Nothing would give me greater joy than for all of us to be in heaven together. I know you may not become Christians, but I promise you, I will love you, serve you, and be here for you."

When the service was over, the hallways were so crammed with people, it was hard to move. But we ate and enjoyed ourselves. I was swarmed by so many people, it was hard to talk to everyone. I remember one man from Yemen, who'd brought a lot of people with him to the event, saying, "See, I brought you the world tonight!" Person after person came up to me, thanking the church for reaching out. I was especially moved by meeting the young Muslim fathers. One after another said it was hard raising their children as Muslims in Dallas, trying to break out of the box as we were doing. I wasn't ready for that; it really broke my heart. And I still remember how surreal it was watching our Northwood children play with kids from different backgrounds wearing different clothing.

It was surreal, and one reason was that the whole time this gathering was taking place, my wife and her friend were in the West Bank working with Muslim women building bridges and relationships—not with the church there, but with the people there who were not Christians. They were the minority there in the West Bank working with Muslims, while our church at home was the majority religion in our city reaching out to the minority.

Fallout and Reach Out

The fallout of this service was incredible. For example, in the foyer there was a table that had been left set up from Sunday morning, where church members could sign up for service projects in the inner city. Some Muslim families went to the table and started signing up! A church member ran over and asked me, "What should we do?"

I told him, "Let them sign up!" Now the number of service projects we do with one another continues to grow as people are becoming friends.

The gathering was picked up all over the world as people watched the service on the Web. Between Dallas and abroad, the comments spoke of the deep desire for this type of thing.

A European diplomat wrote, "You earned the admiration and respect of Europeans like me, who may not turn to God as frequently but recognize the truth in your courageous initiative. If faith does not allow for that, what good is it?"

A Muslim man in the DFW area wrote, "I'd like to express and share, with you and everyone else, my uncontained pleasure on the successful event . . . I have been involved in interfaith activities for the last thirty-five years in the United States and never saw or heard about any such Muslim–Christian event of this nature and magnitude."

A Northwood member wrote, "I can't sleep, and images of Sunday night keep flashing before my mind. I believe God is speaking something powerful to me and our church through last night's event."

A Northwood mother wrote, "I'm so grateful our three kids got to be a part of this historic act of God . . . It was and still is out of my comfort zone. God has opened my heart in ways I didn't know possible."

When I reflect back on this event, the word that comes most to mind is *honor*. The Muslims walking in our church were smiling, heads held high, and they greeted us and one another as if they felt respected. And they were. They were honored and they appreciated it. They were so hungry for relationships and friendships.

We continue to plan similar events, small and large. Anyone can do it, really. It's as simple as going to lunch or a movie with someone, or just sitting in your yard talking to a neighbor. At first, I knew Zia as a Muslim and as an imam, as the gatekeeper to his people. Now I know him as a man and as a friend. I'm convinced the greatest value of Christian pastors and Muslim imams is not their debates on scripture, but the ability to connect their congregations in healthy relationships in a connected world and city. Religious leaders want to sit around and debate God and truth, but if they connect their followers, those debates become far more meaningful.

Again, I want to remind us all that many Muslims don't want to be isolated from American values or Christians. Al Jazeera, the Arab broadcast station, invited me to a meeting in Doha a few months ago, at which I got to meet with many of the young revolutionaries of the Arab Spring, men from Egypt, Tunisia, Libya, Syria, and other places. I listened to their stories and enjoyed having meals with them and hanging out. These young men had caught the older Islamists—who had been working for regime change for years from an Islamic perspective of political control—by surprise. The younger ones took to the streets and challenged things. One of their most important weapons was and is social media; because of the Web, they could see what the rest of the world is like.

During the meeting one old Islamist was trashing the young revolutionaries, saying they were immature in their thinking and had no strong philosophy of leadership. The divide at the conference between the young and the old was huge. Then one young revolutionary said, "We do have a philosophy, and it's the philosophy of human rights! Furthermore, we don't want to trade one dictator for another dictator, even if he is religious. The greatest threat we have is the little dictator that lives inside all our hearts."

There is much to unpack in that response, but one thing it says to me is that many people across the globe, including Muslims, don't want to be isolated. They want to connect with the rest of the world and experience different cultures and build relationships. Another thing it suggests: America's founding fathers gave us something that will work for the whole world—religious freedom and human rights. Suppressing religion is old-school, and it's simply a matter of time until repressive regimes lighten up. As Americans we must continue to model freedom of religion. Our faith was made for the public square. We don't have to lack confidence or retreat; it's been tested and validated for centuries.

And as American Christians, we should live it out in a way that demonstrates not just tolerance but genuine love, showing the world how to get along in a pluralistic society. When I travel, I love to jog in the major cities I visit. When I jog, I see people and the city in such a different way, seeing life as it is at street level, as opposed to being shuttled from one place to the next in taxis or planes. It's time we get out of the taxis and off the planes. Instead of driving by one another, I want us to engage in relationships with one another at the street level.

Are you ready to stop living in isolation as a follower of Jesus? He needs you out there, connecting with and loving people. People are hungry for relationships, especially from the other side of the world. Ask God to open your eyes and heart to people. Are you ready to extend your hand?

FOUR

SERVING OTHERS WITH ALL MY MIGHT

Let your light shine before others, so that they may see your good works and give glory to your Father who is in heaven.

—Matthew 5:16

Greater love has no one than this, that someone lay down his life for his friends.

—John 15:13

Compete with one another in good works.

—from the Quran

A friend who was doing work in Afghanistan asked if Northwood Church could do in Afghanistan some of the things we were doing in Vietnam, so I agreed to come and talk about it. Being all manly and from Texas, I can grow a beard fast. So I grew it out and, with a couple of buddies, headed for Afghanistan. In Pakistan, we bought Afghan clothes and crossed the border into Afghanistan. We found a place to stay for the first night, and then went straight to the office of the governor of the province.

There we met with an official, and I told him, "My name is Bob Roberts, and I pastor a church in Dallas, Texas. I am sorry for all the pain and hardship your country is going through, and want to try to help any way that I can. I won't preach, pass out tracts, or do religious work— I will only serve your people, if you like. If someone does ask me about my faith, I won't deny it, and I will answer questions honestly, but that is all. If you want me to come, let me know."

He thanked me for being honest and forthright with him and said they needed help with many things. He gave me a list of projects to look at. I kept stressing I was there to explore, that I didn't have anything in mind yet;

I was just trying to see what was possible. He mentioned they needed some clinics and a children's hospital.

I'm not an Episcopalian or Presbyterian—I didn't know anyone with $10 million to build a children's hospital. So I got on the phone and called every Presbyterian and Episcopalian I could. And I found one—a man who builds children's hospitals around the world—and he wound up going to Afghanistan and starting a hospital there.

Later we had a groundbreaking ceremony for the new facility, and when it was over we went back to the house we were staying at to talk. As we sat on the floor in Afghan style around the rug, I said to the guy beside me, "I'd love to hike in these mountains here and really see this place!"

A man opposite me, who was Pashtun, heard me and said, "Bob Roberts, you want to see Afghanistan, I show you Afghanistan!" I leaned over to my friend I was with and asked, "Is it safe here?"

He replied, "Bob, you're in Afghanistan; nothing is safe! But do you know who he is?"

My friend told me the Pashtun man was the son of one of the top tribal leaders of all Afghanistan and that he was a very significant man. He was a few years younger than me, and I had noticed on this trip that anytime we had a snag or something wasn't going smoothly, he'd get on his cell phone and the next thing we knew, everything was going fine. I didn't understand or know exactly who he was, but he seemed nice enough, and we had talked a little.

I told him, "Okay, let's do it."

The man, whose name is Umer, replied, "Good, we will have fun, and I will show you Afghanistan!" He grabbed my backpack, and I jumped in the middle seat of the SUV. He was driving with a machine gunner beside him. I sat behind him catty-corner, with a machine gunner beside me. In the back compartment was a man with a rocket launcher. Now, I'm from East Texas, and as I've said, we love to shoot guns and hunt deer. I've run deer with dogs on hunts. But I've got to tell you, it doesn't come close to comparing with camel chasing across the desert with a rocket launcher. That was one of the wildest things I've ever done in my entire life. Yes, we really did it. *No*, I didn't get one, but it was sure fun to shoot.

We finally got to his family's compound a couple of hours later. I didn't realize where we were at the time, but we had entered a province in which Al Qaeda had trained. We were on the backside of a desert with mountains all around; it was beautiful. They knew I was from Texas, so thinking I was a cowboy, they brought out a camel for me to ride. I didn't do so well and fell in some camel crap (no one says dung—make it real). Everyone laughed, me included.

We were still laughing when Umer said, "Okay Bob, I show you more of Afghanistan!"

"No, Umer, this is enough, really," I replied.

"No, Bob. You no worry; just don't talk." He didn't know what he was asking of me.

So we got back into the SUV, and he drove me to the little village where he grew up. He told me how they needed a school there. He asked if I'd be open to helping build one. He really didn't need my help; he had and has far more money than I ever will. It was a gesture. So I said, "Sure, I'll take care of it." It would cost only ten grand, and I knew I could raise that somehow.

As we continued to travel, I became a little concerned. We were out in the middle of nowhere. He knew very little of me. I knew less of him. Was this safe? I asked him, "Umer, in Pashtun culture, my understanding is if I'm you're guest, then you have to protect me whether you like me or not, whether I'm good or bad. Is this true?"

"Yes, Bob Roberts, this is true."

Realizing the leadership role of his tribe, I pushed the envelope and asked, "So, if bin Laden has been in Afghanistan, you would have to protect him as well. You met him, right?"

"You very funny man, Bob Roberts, very funny!"

That's all he ever said about bin Laden. "So even if I am Christian, you have to protect me, right?" I repeated. He said, "Of course, I assume you are, you are American."

I asked him, "So Umer, do you know what I do?"

"Yes," he replied, "you are a humanitarian."

I told him, "Yes, I am humanitarian, but do you know what I do in America; do you know who funds the humanitarian work and how I do it?" He didn't know.

"I am a Christian pastor."

He was silent a second and said, "Okay."

I asked him, "Do you know what a pastor is?" He didn't understand, so I said, "I'm like a Christian imam."

"No, you cannot be, you laugh too much, Bob Roberts!"

I said, "No, it's true. That's really what I do."

He started smiling and said, "This is very good." He got on his satellite phone and made a call and said, "I will have very good special surprise for you tonight."

I didn't know if it would be fried Baptist preacher or what. We drove on in the desert, as he showed me the area.

When we got to one village, Umer did something that changed the course of my life. He began to brag that I would help build a school in his village. Immediately, the young imams began to ask if I would build some for their villages as well. I didn't know what to do or what to say. These were Muslims. They believed in the *dawah*, which means, *invite people to Islam*. I believe in the Great Commission, which is to make Jesus known to all peoples. Would this be a compromise of my faith? Would I be hurting the Great Commission?

But then I began to think if I ever was going to work

in these villages, I would have to go through the local imam, and here they were. I wanted the whole world to follow Jesus, but I didn't know what to do. I remember saying in my head, *WWPD—what would Paul do?* What did Paul do? Paul always spoke with respect to people of other faiths. Paul started in the synagogues. Paul complimented the people at Mars Hill. Paul built relationships. I didn't have anyone to call and ask what I should do. I had to respond one way or the other.

I took a deep breath and in my heart prayed, "Jesus, I sense you have opened this door and I'm going through it. If I'm sinning, make me stop. Let me get blown up if this is wrong. I want to do nothing wrong here. But unless you do that, I will move forward."

I began to think of young pastors in America I was trying to persuade to work internationally and thought maybe some of them would come here. So I said, "Okay, I'll do it." But I also wanted to make sure some of the values that Christians bring to the table were honored. So I added, "But here's what we will do. We will build the schools. In the meantime, you read the New Testament, and we will read the Quran—to get to know each other's faith better. And when we build the school, 25 percent of the students have to be girls." I knew this was one way to bring greater equality to that society, even if it was a small step by American standards.

Then I said, "And what if I get a Christian imam to come and work here, to work with you and become friends with you?" They loved it! They asked, "Would American Christian imams be *willing* to come here and work with us?" I told them, "I'll bet I could find a couple."

And we did just that. That led to many other projects in Afghanistan as well. The result wasn't just the clinics, schools, or agricultural projects, but the relationships that were developed.

That night they prayed, and I knelt behind them on a knee and prayed to Jesus. I slept well under those stars.

How to Connect with Muslims

I've been encouraging you to get involved with people of other faiths. I've given hints here and there about how to do it. In this chapter, I want to become a little more specific. The experience I had in Afghanistan may seem exotic, but it illustrates how anyone anywhere can reach out beyond his own tribe. How can we be bold in love toward others?

We need to begin by remembering the driving motive behind our reaching out: the universal love of God as expressed in the Great Commission. We are called to go to the uttermost parts of the earth to spread the good news of God's love, though sometimes, as we've seen, that means sharing God's love with those parts of the earth that have come to live in our own communities. However, we need to take this idea one step further than we usually do.

Early missions taught us about the nations, the peoples, their cultures, their beliefs and worldviews—and of course, how to share our faith with people in different lands. But it also assumed that some people would go out in missions to other parts of the world, and the rest of us would pray and pay for them to do so. Missions was something other people did; we learned about it through slide shows and the occasional short-term missions trip.

I love what David Platt has written in his book *Radical*, in which he calls Christians to make big financial sacrifices for the sake of others. The greatest sacrifice, however, is not our living in less square footage or driving a Honda instead of a BMW, but *our willingness to actually go and engage*, to share the good news of Jesus with people who do not know him.

One thing we'll have to do is begin to place this type of missions at the center of our faith, not the periphery. I was with a group of pastors talking about how hard it is to focus outside their own cities and local churches. To drive home my point, I asked them, "When you lead someone to Jesus, how much of the gospel do you give him? What if you told him, 'You have to stop the affair, but a little pornography is okay?'" I asked them if they would ever tell anyone that.

"Of course not," they responded.

But that's the sort of thing we do with the Great Commission. We say, "Become a Christian, grow in your faith, and sometime somewhere down the line, we'll talk about reaching out to others." Instead, we should be encouraging one another to integrate the Great Commission into the very core of our identity as Christians. Jesus began his call to the apostles to follow him to be fishers of men before they even knew who he was.

No generation in the history of humanity has had more opportunity, and therefore none will have as much accountability as we will when we stand before God. You can read about what part of that looks like to me in my books *Glocalization* and *Real-Time Connections*. I believe every disciple—every member of the body of Christ—should use his vocation to serve humanity while sharing Jesus. We shouldn't *do* church; we should *be* the church on the grid of society. The Great Commission will not be fulfilled because we raise up more preachers and missionaries like me, but because we raise up disciples who are willing to be the church every day.

With that as the overriding perspective, we can start to talk about practical ways to reach out to people of other faiths.

Start with the Hand

When we build a relationship with someone, start with the hand. That is: serve him. Most people focus on head, heart, and then hand. I believe just the opposite. We first start with the hand.

We sweat together and we talk about our families; we simply get to know each other. Now we've captured his heart and made a friend of him.

Once we've moved from hand to heart and established trust, we can talk about what we think; we begin to understand each other. Talking without first trusting leads to endless and fruitless debates. Talking *with* trust leads to genuine and deep conversations. I never have a single conversation to "finish the deal." It's many conversations. I grew up in a culture of manufacturing converts: share the facts and get them to pray the prayer. I'm not sure most of those people really understood what they were praying.

Most of us start with the head, and we get nowhere, because we have no relationship of trust to convey that we genuinely care and don't view this person as a pawn in some religious game we are playing. When we start with the head and have a conversation about God too quickly, it becomes an argument. That never works. We wind up debating our views, and the result is we divide too quickly and don't go deep in relationship.

When we start with the hand, especially on a project for the common good that we can join around and do together, we can have deep conversations. Each faith is allowed to stand on its own merits and be seen for what it is in the lives of those who follow it. Even the Puritans had a concept by which they could work together for the common good, even with those who were not Christians but who might have shared some common values. And there are many similarities between Christian and Islamic values: concern for the poor, the importance of the family, and so forth. Once we sweat together, we become friends. Trust is established.

We sometimes don't realize how crucial trust is—not just in relationships but to heal the broken places of the earth. Non-Christians are used to empty promises from this group or that. Who's for real? How can they tell if we are? Only sweat equity will tell them how serious we are. From there we become friends and our hearts get engaged. Now we're ready to talk.

KISS: Keep It Simple Service

Sometimes people want a strategy for engaging their neighbors. I saw a tweet recently by a friend that went something like this: "Stop sweating over all this; just hang out with some people you need to serve and let it happen."

That's exactly right. When you get to know a next-door neighbor, do you need a class for it? Of course not. You bake a pie, mow his grass, invite him to a game, or do whatever. *That's all you need to do.* You don't have to have the answer to every question. Just start where you are.

Here are some guidelines you and your churches can use as you engage globally and locally:

- Use charity only for a crisis, not long-term engagement. Charity can actually get in the way of development. Historically, the church and Christians throw money at poverty. But we now know it's better to build a factory or some kind of work center to provide jobs, build the economy, and establish the community, rather than to offer a one-time donation to put some food on a plate. In the case of a tsunami, earthquake, or other natural disaster, we all need to work together for charity, but not for everyday living. Serving a neighbor in a crisis or hard time is important, but we need a relationship that goes beyond crisis to deep sharing. Charity is giving to the poor. In a disaster we must be charitable. But in cities and societies that are poor and impoverished, charity can actually keep people enslaved. Instead of giving money, producing jobs through factories, micro-finance, and other projects enable people to have jobs.

- Focus on a place long-term; this builds acceptance and credibility. When we do "dine and dash" ministry, it reinforces negative stereotypes the world has about us. Our church focuses on Vietnam and Mexico. We've been in Vietnam since 1995; having a presence there that long has huge implications for serving the city and being connected to leaders. Many times churches will focus on a new place every year (if not multiple places). What if all the volunteers and resources were brought to bear on a single city for several years? The impact would be dramatic.

- As individuals, we should connect in the domains (education, economics, medical, civil society, agriculture, communication, governance, plumbing, carpentry, dentistry—whatever our line of work) that we already serve in. Don't focus on religious work. Focus on the needs of the city. Cities and nations operate on domains, the natural infrastructures all societies are built upon. Most Christians think in terms of hosting Bible studies. While that may be good, there is so much more that we have to offer, like using our personal skill sets to serve humanity in the name of Jesus. People really don't care that much that we have a Bible study, but over the long term they might become interested in the Jesus in whose name we serve.

- Leave ideas and programs at home; instead, let domain leaders connect and design based on expertise and need. Most churches design mission outreaches back in the mission departments, but that day is over. Our strategies should be centered around the connections people make in their lives on a daily basis, and we should be serving in our own domains and networks based on *our* daily lives.

- Go on missions as global partners, not as the "Great Savior." People don't want to be treated as charity cases. Many Christians today are getting into the "missional" mind-set. I like a lot of what it means, but there is still a lot to learn. Most Christians who engage do a project *for* the community, not *with* the community. It's like we Christians show up as a tribe in our white hats, saying all the while, "Look at us." But we are a part of the community, and therefore should not isolate ourselves from it. When we do, it smacks of arrogance and religious colonialism.

- Pray to be filled with the Holy Spirit every day. Divine appointments and opportunities to be the hands and feet of Jesus are all around us, and they will come in simple, unexpected ways. Many people are thinking of big events and opportunities, but the greatest fulfillment will come from the individual relationships we make along the way.

The events we've had at our church are not debates or education seminars; they are meet-and-greet sessions. The pilgrimage to the three houses of worship, the Global Faith Forum, the Building Bridges event—all served as mixers to help people get to know one another. Yes, we stated what we believe, but we didn't debate each other. Once we had established preliminary relationships, we then focused on things we could do together that would let us serve our city. There was the cooking club, working at a seniors center, rebuilding and refurbishing homes, getting together just for fun—all of these things started opening the door to developing legitimate friendships.

For example, when Nikki's father became extremely ill, several of the Muslim women got together and sent some gifts to him. They also told Nikki they would be praying. That meant a tremendous amount to Nikki. Her dad loved it.

Likewise, the father of one of the Muslim women also got ill, but he lived in Detroit. A young couple from our church had their friends in Detroit go by and check up on the woman's father.

I have a friend from Syria who told me, "In the West you marry the one you love, but in the Middle East we love the one we marry." There's a lot of truth in that way of doing marriage. Love is a choice, not an emotion. When we serve others, we start not with emotion but with commitment to serve in the name of Jesus. If we build service and caring based on emotion, we won't make it. But if we do it in the name of Jesus and we do it for him and because we love him, we won't give up. Furthermore, we will come to deeply love the people we serve.

Not long ago someone was with me when I was with a group of Islamic leaders. Afterward he said, "You really love those guys, don't you!" I said, "Yes, but didn't you know that?" He responded, "I never realized how much you cared for them. To you, they really are people, not just potential converts for your religion."

New Friendships

If we start with the hands and keep it simple, it's amazing what can happen, even with the most unexpected people. Let me return to my experience with the Afghans.

I occasionally flew to Afghanistan to see the progress of our work, and sometimes imams would greet me at the airport when I arrived. I became friends with one particular imam, and I always looked forward to going to his village. I came to admire and love this man. We were both genuinely shocked to become friends with one another—one Muslim and one Christian, from different sides of the world.

Then there is my friend Umer, who at the time I write this is a member of the Afghan parliament and on a committee for international relations. He recently sent me a list of things that need to be done to help Afghan villagers.

I have come to love the Afghan people, especially the Pashtuns. They are a lot like Texans. Men like these have enriched my personal faith in ways they couldn't imagine. When we finally got into some deep conversations, they asked me questions I couldn't answer all that easily. They forced me to think more deeply about what I believe. We were forced to be deeply honest with one another.

I had a conversation with one of my Afghan friends, as I did with Imam Zia in Dallas. "So, be honest," I began. "I know you love me. If I die, what happens to me in your way of understanding Islam?"

Zia said, "Well, Bob, it's not that good. I think it's the

same thing you think happens to me for rejecting Jesus as God." He went on to say, "But I want you to know that I do care about you, Bob." He also knows that I care deeply about him.

One day I told him, "I love being able to have a friend in Islam who is honest with me, and we don't have to get upset or feel threatened. Thanks for being real with me." He replied, "I feel the same way, Bob."

Such conversations also brought me closer to my Afghan friends. They were no longer a "people group" to me; these were real, live individuals who had wives, children, and needs I could identify with. I laughed with them; I've had very personal conversations with them. As others became more directly involved in our Afghan work, I began to step away and let others run with it. But I will carry these men in my heart to my grave. I'm not saying I agree with them on politics or religion, or that I wouldn't challenge them from time to time. But I still love them.

This doesn't mean everything is warm and fuzzy. When we really believe the gospel, and we really love someone, we will weep for his or her soul. To pray for "peoples" is important, but to love a specific "person" changes the way we pray. The most important thing to do is not look at the mass of people, but see the person. The person will help us understand the masses. We need to read books to learn about religions, the world, and people. But nothing can take the place of personal relationships

Opening for the Gospel

Late one evening in Afghanistan, the group I was traveling with, which included Umer, arrived in a small village built around an oasis and a spring. It looked like a picture out of Bible times. The houses were made of mud and rock. There were palm trees. It was a very clean village. I'm not sure how many people lived there, maybe a thousand or two. We pulled into the fortlike structure in the middle of the village, with walls about twelve feet high. It was big enough that three SUVs could pull in, and rugs could be thrown on the dirt floor for us to eat and later sleep on. There was no roof, only four walls making a perfect square, and men with machine guns dressed as Pashtun walked the tops of the walls.

We got out of the SUVs and sat on the ground, and food was brought from who knows where. It was incredibly tasty. I got real excited when someone said we were going to have yogurt. I wondered how they were going to get the frozen stuff out there. Sure enough, they brought out a huge bowl of it, made from goat's milk. It was warm, not frozen, and the bowl was passed from one bearded man to the next. It came my time, and with great prayer, I took my big slurp. I winced a little, but smiled, and the men began to laugh. There were maybe ten or so of us, and we had fun laughing and talking for some time.

I thought we were finished, when Umer clapped his hands and said something in Pashto. In came several young men and one older man, all in white robes; they were all imams. Umer served as my translator, and he told them, "I have a special surprise for you. This is Bob Roberts, and he is a Christian imam from America. You can ask him anything you want."

In the course of the evening, I walked them through the Old Testament—the five books of Moses, wisdom literature, major prophets, minor prophets, and so forth. I then took them through the New Testament and explained the Gospels, the epistles. I then explained the core beliefs of Christianity. I'd never explained so much with any Muslim. I asked them questions as well. I don't know how long we talked that night, but it was very late.

Serving others and serving with others is the gospel in action. And it opens doors to not only friendships, but crucial conversations like this, during which we can share the story of salvation with others.

Some Christians argue that serving takes the place of sharing the gospel. I disagree. Serving is the core of how the gospel is expressed; it's what Matthew 25 says we will be judged on: feeding, giving water, providing shelter, addressing issues of justice. The early church had a reputation of sharing and hospitality, and it grew because of it. Loving is showing and telling. Telling without showing is cold and manipulative. Showing without telling is merely humans showing compassion with no divinity. We must use both.

Even if others choose not to accept Jesus, the world is a better place when we serve others. It builds relational capital, and that enables us to treat one another with respect. God is glorified when men are at peace.

We have a saying at Northwood: "Serve not to convert, but serve because you've been converted." We can't save anyone anyhow—only God does that. We aren't serving to talk men into becoming Christians. The Spirit of God draws men. We are living the life of Christ before men, serving them because it's what Jesus did and does. As one of our teenagers once said, "We don't have to 'pimp' the gospel, God does it." God is big enough to save and keep what is his.

Some churches are getting bad reputations globally because they are using world crises—like tsunamis and massive earthquakes—not to serve humanity but to try to convert them. I want people to accept Christ, but it all goes back to serving because we've been converted, not in order to convert others. If we serve, there will be plenty of chances to share our faith.

A Witness in a Tough Place

This hasn't been just my experience, but the experience of many other Christians who have changed the way they relate to Muslims. The paradox is that the less we try to convert, and simply serve, the more Muslims are interested in the Christian faith.

Take the example of a minister I'll call Joseph. He pastors in the heart of a city full of Muslims, and he has seen his church grow to some twenty thousand believers. I interviewed him on my blog, and here is what he said:

Joseph, do you fear Muslims?

No, I don't fear Muslims.

Why?

They are human beings like me. They are also a creation of God.

Do you have friends that are Muslims?

I have a lot of friends, even the mayor of the city. He's a Muslim. Even the members of Parliament, even the chairman of the imams for the country is my friend.

How should Christians respond to Muslims?

They need to love them. They should show them they also have value no matter how they believe.

In the early days, you had some Muslims persecute you.

They went as far as burning my house when some people were going to be baptized.

Were you afraid of them?

At that time very much. I thought they would kill me.

What changed that?

I had to make a strong relationship with them and their leaders. I discovered what I was lacking was love to the Muslim people. That was a problem!

What is your relationship like with Muslims now?

We can come together and discuss issues concerning our nation and our community without arguing about each people's faith.

Do you ever discuss your faith with imams and Muslims?

I discuss with them about my faith, and they do the same. We remain friends because we respect each other's faith.

You do a lot of city engagement projects. What are some of the things you do?

I have started their school, [for students] from kindergarten to high school. [We've also sponsored] orphanages, compassionate projects, water projects to serve the community, regardless of their faith.

What would you say to Christians about how to relate to Muslims, especially if they don't know any but live where they are?

We have to understand that Jesus loves everyone. The love of Christ is in our life. To demonstrate that love, we must have a relationship with others.

As Christians who are interested in serving others, we should consider our jobs and other points of connection we have within our communities, such as people who help prepare taxes for inner-city people, landscapers building corrals in Vietnam for water buffalo, people tutoring kids in public schools. Making a list of everywhere we go and everything we do helps broaden our thinking. Then we can make a list of people we see in these places and during these activities who are from different religions or have a different lifestyle. Most people avoid them, but how are we going to serve them? This is simple love and radical obedience, which allows us to be salt and light right where we are.

FIVE

REQUIRING ALL MY TRUTH

I am the way, and the truth, and the life. No one comes to the Father except through me.

—John 14:6

For God so loved the world, that he gave his only Son, that whoever believes in him should not perish but have eternal life.

—John 3:16

"So why do you Christians believe in three gods?" a Muslim once asked me.

"We don't," I replied. "We believe in just one God."

"But you have the Father, the Son Jesus, and the Holy Spirit!"

I was sitting in Doha at an Al Jazeera global conference. A young lady who is a part of the Muslim Brotherhood from Egypt wanted an explanation. I had just answered her question about Protestants and Catholics, and then about all the denominations. Now she wanted to know more: she wanted core theology, and I was the only Christian she knew to ask.

At the table were a Jewish man who had been the head of AIPAC (American Israel Public Affairs Committee) for twelve years, and his wife, who was a secularist. Other Muslims from around the world were also at the table, all looking at me. But I was fine with her question. I had been asked it many times before and had come to think deeply about my answer. When I explained the Trinity as best as I could, they didn't become believers on the spot, but they did say, "That makes sense. We understand now why that's important to you Christians."

Experiences like this remind me why we have to

move from theology being a discipline for religious leaders to something everyday believers can understand and talk about. It isn't enough to explain theology to believers; believers are going to have to explain theology to nonbelievers when asked.

No Luxury

I didn't come to this view easily. I've always had a love-hate relationship with theology. As I once wrote on my blog:

> More than anything *I love God*, and I love spending time with him, being his child, serving him. *I love the Bible.* I read through it every year and read several books again and again to study and reflect. *I love worship*, the ability to encounter God either privately or in a public setting. *I love ministry* that is glocal, touching lives locally and globally. *I love the adventure* of following God in the moment, of recognizing his voice and then doing what he says. But I have to be honest: I really get *frustrated with theology.*

That's because we often make theology so complicated we take the life out of it. We divorce it from everyday life so that it means nothing to most people.

Even pastors, educated at seminaries, can be intimidated by theology. Sometimes when I speak to groups of pastors, I ask them how confident they are in sharing their faith. Nearly every hand in the room will go up. I then ask, "Are you just as confident in explaining the Trinity?" Few hands go up. I believe we need to do better than this. We don't have to have all the answers, but we all, pastors and lay people, should feel confident talking about the basics of our faith.

Theology is simply a word that means *the study of God.* Systematic theology is a way of understanding God in a consistent framework. *Everyone* has theology. You can't say, "I have no theology," because even in saying that, you espouse a theology. I love reading J. I. Packer, John Stott, Martyn Lloyd-Jones, John Piper, N. T. Wright, J. Dwight Pentecost, Dallas Willard, Gordon Fee, E. Stanley Jones, Ben Witherington, Don Carson, Dietrich Bonhoeffer, and the list goes on. Though I disagree with each of them at different points, they have taught me a lot in their books, lectures, and lives.

One reason we're afraid of talking with people of other faiths is that we might be asked a question we can't answer or don't understand ourselves. We don't want to be embarrassed. But we needn't fear—most people are just as uninformed in their faith as we are in ours. We must get away from this idea that we have to find experts or give away a book in order to help others understand our faith. People are going to receive information best from someone they trust, rather than a book written by someone they don't know.

As we get to know our neighbors, they will ask questions. Sure, they could read a book or talk to a pastor, but they would rather ask someone they feel they have a relationship with, someone they believe cares about them.

If I'm asked a question I don't have a good answer to, sometimes I just reply, "Let me do some more homework" or "Let me ask someone else, and I'll get back to you." If I know only part of the answer, I simply say, "Part of the answer is . . . But let me do some more homework and get back to you." People are always grateful to have their questions taken so seriously. We should remember God has brought our lives together, which means God has confidence we can deal with their questions.

One thing multifaith conversations have done for me is this: they've deepened my theology and faith in Christ. I knew little about atheism and why people believed it when I first started working with communists. My learning curve shot up really fast when I encountered atheists who were waiting for answers. So I starting learning for a real purpose with real people, rather than taking a class for something I might use later.

When I first got involved with Muslims, I was a little

intimidated, but as I got into Islam and had to explain my faith, it wasn't nearly as hard as I had thought it would be. I began to read the Quran and found some parts of it were easy to understand and some not so easy.

This is exciting because it's been an opportunity to grow. I've believed in the Trinity my entire ministry and spiritual life, but it's only been in the past few years that I've been this excited about it and able to explain it in a way that makes sense to others. This process has helped me understand why it matters. We're tempted to say the Trinity is a mystery that we can't understand. That's true in part, and it may work for Christians, but it doesn't cut it for a Jew or a Muslim or anyone for whom the Trinity is a real stumbling block to faith. Yes, each explanation of the Trinity has its problems, from the three-leaf clover to water as liquid, solid, and gas. But that doesn't mean we shouldn't try to help others grasp what we believe. The Trinity is no less than our very definition of who God is—that's kind of important. Who is this God we are inviting people to follow? We had better be ready to answer that question.

This isn't a luxury for educated Christians or a pursuit only for those who want to go deeper in their faith. It's a critical thing for everyday followers of Jesus. In the 1970s and 1980s, people began to say they'd had enough with all this theology and they just wanted to know and experience Jesus. We hear the same thing today. Sadly, sometimes we pastors and theologians have made theology so complex that people are intimidated by it; they don't even want to have a conversation about it for fear of saying something wrong. Now we're at the point where people can't explain their faith to others inside or outside the faith.

Part of the problem is how theology is approached, as if it were something senior engineers teach other engineers. And perhaps that's true at the academic level. But at the church level, theology is about studying God in a way that connects to people's lives; most people are not going to read a thousand-page book on systematic theology.

I believe we live in a time when theology is more important than ever before. The greatest theology book has yet to be written for the twenty-first century, and when it is written, it won't be a thousand but 75 to 125 pages in length. Wycliff, Tyndale, and others made the Bible accessible and understandable for the everyday people of fourteenth- and fifteenth-century England. It's time to have a similar explosion of understanding of theology now. Sadly, it's currently a discipline driven by engineers who write manuals for pastor-engineers who teach it in such a way that most people don't know what they are talking about and are too intimidated to even try. If we can't teach people the core basics of our theology and answer their questions in simple ways, we can forget keeping our followers "safe" from other faiths. This isn't true of only Christianity, but of all faiths. It's time to move from complex tribal theology to core global theology.

Moving into Global Theology

What shapes our theology? Of course—the Bible! But what makes us focus on certain parts of the Bible? I think in large measure it has to do with the questions that the Spirit of God is putting on our hearts at various stages of our lives. I think it is important to follow the Spirit's leading here, so that we'll learn what he might teach us.

This is how it has worked for me and why I'm so excited about the emerging global theology.

First, theology for me was about salvation for my friends, not even salvation for me. When I accepted Jesus as my Savior as a teenager, I did so not as a theologian but as a person seeking truth and God in a personal way. My first stab at theology was trying to understand how salvation happens so I could lead my friends to Jesus. It was the theology of the cross and the resurrection and forgiveness of my sin. It was grace and mercy and atonement all wrapped up.

Then theology became about the church and my tribe. Was I to be a preacher and lead a church? At that point in my life, in my twenties, I was concerned about what I believed, how to organize theology, how it all fit together and made sense (systematic theology), and learning the beliefs of my tribe (Baptists). When I found things that didn't fit, I tried to make them fit. I debated about how far to take things like election and free will, the second coming of Christ, the role of the Holy Spirit. All of us believe in these things, but there are nuances to each one. Often, what I believed had little to do with personal experience but much to do with study and what my tribe believed.

A third phase began in my thirties. My theology began to be shaped by how I experienced God. To know about him and understand him in a systematic way is one thing, but to know him personally and experience his fullness and power, that is another. Personal worship took on a new dimension with me; the kingdom of God—not just the restoration of the individual but the reconciliation of all things—and the themes of justice and mercy shaped how I read Scripture. This caused me to read history to understand how the great theologians had developed their theology, and I discovered that much of it had to do with how they experienced God. This was true of Jonathan Edwards, John Calvin, Martin Luther, and others. Their theologies are, in many ways, about the personal God they experienced.

In my forties I began to understand God in a global context like never before. We all say the church is global because of the Great Commission, as if global theology starts and stops with that one verse. It doesn't. The reformers and others taught us things from God's Word that are relevant to this very moment in time. However, they were not comprehensive and complete. God has given his complete revelation in the Word, and today the world is different, with unique opportunities, challenges, and context in which theology is lived out.

To meet those opportunities and challenges, we need a global theology. But what does that look like? Well, to me it has certain features.

Global theology deals with the core issues.

What are the core tenets of our faith (or of another faith we are studying)? Who is God? Who is man? How does man find God and relate to him? What does God expect of us? How do we relate to others? What is sin and how do we overcome it and find forgiveness and peace? How do we walk in our faith? Where is history going? If you know the basic answers to these questions, you are well on your way to doing global theology. These are the questions people are asking, not to write a dissertation, but to find answers to life's deepest questions. Some Christians will want to go deep into theology, and there is certainly the freedom to do so. But first we should shoot for something that is clear and explainable. In the past, catechisms and creeds have helped in this respect, and they still can. But we need to do more than state, "I believe . . ." We also have to know why we believe it.

I happen to like the Lausanne Covenant[1] because it's broad and basic; it's hard to find anything to disagree with. I would keep that or something similar close by as a starting point of what you believe, gradually studying each of the sections.

Global theology is simple.

It has to be easy to explain. Simple does not mean shallow or watered down. Sometimes the simplest things are the most profound. Nothing is simpler than "God loves you." And nothing is more profound than "God loves you." The implications of that love have practical, daily, and eternal consequences.

At our Global Faith Forum in November 2010 (you can see the videos at www.globalfaithforum.org), Prince Turki al-Faisal of Saudi Arabia demonstrated one way of keeping theology simple. For the Friday night session, he was on a panel with professor John Esposito (an expert on Islam) and a couple of others. Each panelist had ten minutes to make a presentation, but John was keynoting the discussion, so he was allotted twenty minutes. Prince Turki told me if John got twenty minutes, he would as well. I thought he was kidding and just laughed. It turned out, he wasn't kidding.

When his turn came, he pulled out the Quran, which had tons of bookmarks in it. He began to read one passage after another, turning carefully to each and every bookmark. I thought, *What is he doing? Do I dare interrupt a prince?*

He wasn't even explaining, just reading and reading and reading. People were fidgeting on the stage. Another panelist, the Vietnamese ambassador, looked lost. I'm sure I looked intense. But the prince kept slowly reading passage after passage, smiling as he did so. I began to notice that every passage was either about Jesus or Mary, the mother of Jesus.

When he finally finished—after about thirty minutes—I said, "Your highness, thank you for reading that. But tell me, *why* did you do that?"

"Bob, I want every evangelical here to know that we Muslims respect, love, and believe in Jesus. You cannot be a good Muslim without believing in him and taking seriously what he said—that's all."

I did want to clarify, so people wouldn't be confused. So I said, "Thank you, Your Highness. I appreciate your words. That's incredible, but you don't believe that he was God, right?"

"Right, but we still believe in him."

His is a good example of keeping theology simple: just reading what a scripture says. That's a good, simple place to begin a theology discussion.

Global theology is honest.

I must tell it like it is. When I'm asked hard questions about my faith that can be controversial or seem politically incorrect, I do my best to stay calm, smile, and answer the question honestly.

During one meeting of Christian and Muslim leaders at our church, the conversation turned to the uniqueness of Christ, and I said, "As a Christian, I really do believe Jesus is the only way—not because I feel I am better than others, but because Jesus himself said, 'I am the way, and the truth, and the life. No one comes to the Father except through me'" (John 14:6).

A Muslim participant asked me if that meant I believed everyone who doesn't believe in Jesus goes to hell.

I responded, "Anyone of any religion—Christianity included—who does not accept Jesus as the way, the sacrifice, and the one who brings forgiveness of sin according to the Bible, goes to hell." I said it as pleasantly as I could, took a deep breath, and braced for whatever would come. A Muslim man said, "I like this guy. You know what? My faith teaches me that you're going to hell too. I can work with you. You are at least honest about what you believe."

Most Christians do not realize the high regard for Jesus that Muslims have. Muslims believe Jesus was born of a virgin, but not that God was his Father. They believe he performed miracles. They believe he was a prophet from God. They even believe he is coming back. I was once sitting in the home of the Grand Mufti of Jerusalem at the top of the Mount of Olives and I could see the Eastern gate of Jerusalem. I told him, "You know, we Christians believe Jesus is coming back and will enter that gate."

He said, "We Muslims believe it as well." For Muslims, however, his return is not as the King of kings but only as a prophet proclaiming Islam is the way.

Global theology is not speculative.

We need to stay with the core message. When we focus on speculative things, we actually wind up doing damage to the gospel.

Most Muslims and Arabs think evangelical Christians hate them—but love Jews. That's because some evangelical Christians believe in dispensational premillennialism, a very detailed interpretation of what is going to happen in the end times. It's not a view all Christians adopt, partly because it requires a particular way of reading and understanding the Bible. This view—which I believe is speculative—is getting in the way of evangelizing a whole bunch of people in the world.

I believe Jesus is coming again, and I believe we need

to tell people this is what's going to happen in the end. We need to be prepared to meet God. But the specifics of how and when and where—that's all speculative. If you want to go there, and if beliefs about that help you, fine. But when we're doing theology for others, especially those outside the faith, we need to avoid speculation.

Global theology has focused apologetics.

Apologetics is a discipline that helps us explain the reasons for our faith. It is a discipline more necessary than ever these days.

On a trip to Vietnam, I had a conversation with one of the top leaders of the country. He had done his homework, and somehow he had learned I had a doctorate degree. So he asked me, "Why would any intelligent man believe there is a God?"

Unfortunately, I had slept through most philosophical apologetics. Raised in East Texas, we were taught there are two reasons why we believe God exists: (1) the Bible says so, and (2) we could feel him in our hearts. If we didn't believe or experience that, then we were just making excuses. That may work in a predominately Christian culture, but it does not work in a global culture, and definitely not an atheistic culture.

But God gave me great recall of what I had learned in that class, and I walked the man through the seven philosophical reasons for belief in God. He told me he had never heard anything like that. He asked if I would be willing to come back and share it with his friends, who were other top leaders in Vietnam. I eventually did so, and they, too, were fascinated. One of them asked if I would be willing to bring some Bibles to the country and discuss these things. I told him I couldn't. He asked why. I told him the government wouldn't let me do that. That's when he said, "We are the government!"

I hadn't realized to whom I was speaking!

Three Questions

Let me outline three different types of conversations I've had over and over. Allow me to show how I try to answer the basic questions people of no faith or other faiths have asked me. Take the question from my friend in Vietnam: Why do I believe in God at all?

Why do you believe in God?

The seven reasons that make the most sense to me are:

1. Creation. The odds of everything we know of this planet of the universe happening by accident—well, the odds are simply too huge.
2. Form and order. Creation isn't random. The

more we study it, the more we see how everything fits together in all sorts of ways.

3. Diversity, but interdependence of life forms.
To have diversity is one thing. To have interdependence is another. To have both—that
defies the odds.

4. The complexity of creation. There is simply too
much complexity in the design of everything to
believe it is all random. This is what scientist
Francis Collins says led him to believe in God.

5. Uniqueness of man. Biologically, man may
be an animal, but mentally, emotionally, and
morally, he is like no other animal. His ability to create, order, and dominate the world
is unlike any other animal. Random selection
can't explain this.

6. Morality of man. Granted, there are various
types of morality in men, but there is a generally accepted moral code among all tribes of
man—no murder, no stealing, no lying, and
familial fidelity, to name a few. This moral
code comes from somewhere, and can't be
explained by evolution. This was a major argument of C. S. Lewis.

7. Spirituality of man. Man is a spiritual creature.
All spirituality comes from something greater

than biology, something beyond it. All cultures of man have always believed in some form of god(s) regardless of what and how that is defined. Again, evolution can't adequately explain this phenomenon.

Why do you believe in only one God?

This is a question one might be asked mostly in a Hindu context, since Hindus believe in many gods. Here's how I reply:

I have two fundamental choices. Am I a polytheist or monotheist? How I answer this question is critical. This is the question that got Socrates in trouble. As a Greek, in a Greek polytheist culture, and as a philosopher, he concluded there could only be one God. Why?

FIRST, LOGIC. Since there is form and order, design and complexity, it cannot be on account of the whims of many gods who war with each other or jockey for power and control. Forget man blowing himself up; the gods will do it for him.

SECOND, THE UNIFIED LAWS OF NATURE. There is a consistency in science and all knowledge, a sense of a universal knowledge and power that's holding it all together. There is supreme and consistent and unified design that suggests a single power and will behind it.

THIRD, THE CONSISTENT DEVELOPMENT OF HUMANITY HISTORICALLY, SCIENTIFICALLY, AND CULTURALLY. This suggests that that all mankind has the same destiny, suggesting, again, a single grand power or will guiding that history.

I sometimes say more than this, but this is generally how I go about answering this question.

Why are you a Christian? Or, why do you believe in the Trinity?

These are variations of the same question, because to be a Christian means to believe in the Trinity. Now, as I said above, we must talk about Trinity, but we must do so in ways that are not speculative. We need to talk about the Trinity in the context of people's lives and concerns.

To talk about the Trinity, of course, we have to talk about Jesus. In one of my blogs, I once wrote:

> The biggest disagreement I have with Islam is the whole question of who is Jesus. For the Jew, it's who is Jesus. For the Buddhist, it's who is Jesus. For the Hindu, it's who is Jesus. For the Animist, it's who is Jesus. For the Atheist, it's who is Jesus. Why am I going to run down tons of paths without starting with the central question? If we disagree, we disagree, but I refuse to ignore that question.

So let me return to the story I began this chapter with, in which I was asked to explain the Trinity. Here is one way I talk about it:

It may sound like we Christians believe in three gods, but it's not true: we believe in one God.

God the Father created all things—you, me, the world, and all that exists. The book of Genesis teaches us that. Man was God's greatest creation, and he was made in the image of God, because God was building an eternal family. Genesis also teaches us that man fell when he chose sin over God. Now man is separated from God.

Most religions teach that the way a man reaches God now is to do good deeds. This is why God gave us his law and the Ten Commandments in the Hebrew scriptures, or Old Testament. But the law was never meant to save us, only to show us how we couldn't reach God on our own.

The Father is holy and righteous and can't look on our sin, nor can he touch anything sinful. So the Father sent the Word. The gospel of John teaches us that Jesus is the Word, and he was present and part of creation, so he was also God. But when he came to earth, he came as the perfect and complete God-Man.

It was important that he be both. Because he was

man, he could identify with us, what we go through; he could understand the consequences and pain of our sin. As a man, he lived a sinless life, and that was important because to be a worthy sacrifice, one that would really deal with our sins, someone had to fulfill all the requirements of the law. When he went to the cross to die for our sins, he did it as a perfect man. He paid the penalty for our sins.

Because he was God, not just a man, he was raised from the dead—sin couldn't hold him. So by the power of the Holy Spirit, he was raised from the dead, and now sits with God in heaven.

Now Jesus expects us to live like him—he was the pattern of how we are all to live. But we aren't perfect, and won't be until we die and put on a new body. Until then, he continues to be the God-Man before the Father, who sent the Holy Spirit to live in us to give us the power to follow him in our lives.

The point of the Trinity isn't three gods, but God remaining God, not violating his nature and character, while bridging the gap to man so man can be forgiven, live like God wants him to live, and have a relationship with God.

When I gave this answer to one group, someone afterward came up to me and said, "You know, I wish that were true. No wonder so many people are Christians. To know you are forgiven and can go to heaven for sure—that's a really good religion."

The New Focus

Of course, when I talk about these things like this, I always go back to Isaiah 55:8, in which God says, "My thoughts are not your thoughts, neither are your ways my ways." God is not tied to a system or our way of thinking or understanding him. He's God, he's big, he's mysterious. He's self-disclosed, but not totally disclosed. Whatever theology we follow, we must be incredibly careful not to limit him. On the other hand, to ignore theology is to ignore the questions and concerns people all over the world have about God.

When I see theology from the first three phases of theology I went through, I see God one way. But when I read the Bible globally, and see God at work and present in the whole world, it changes everything. Formerly my conversation was mostly about the church and how to start new ones. I still have a heart for planting churches, and in fact, worldwide, Christians are planting new churches at a higher rate than any other time in history. I praise God for that.

But today my focus isn't on establishing churches as much as it is making disciples to go out into the world, using their gifts and skills in society as followers of Jesus. Most of us know how to do religious and church work. Now we need to learn how to live faith in a global, multicultural, multinational, multitribal way. And we need to learn how to talk about that faith—theology—in a way that connects with people all over the globe. We give the plan of salvation in a way people in a Christian culture can get it. That's not enough.

I encourage you to go out today and buy Wayne and Elliot Grudem's brief and concise *Christian Beliefs: Twenty Basics Every Christian Should Know* and begin your study. Christian theology is beautifully summarized in John 3:16: "For God so loved the world, that he gave his only Son, that whoever believes in him should not perish but have eternal life." Explain that theologically to someone; it's a great starting point. Bold love requires us to reach out to love others, but it also requires us to reach deep within the faith we believe to understand it so that when asked we can give every man an answer. We don't need to talk as engineers and professors explaining the faith, but as practitioners of the faith and followers of Jesus. When they see us live it, and then hear us explain it, there is incredible power in that.

One of my favorite passages on this is Colossians 4:3–6, which reads, "At the same time, pray also for us, that God may open to us a door for the word, to declare the mystery of Christ, on account of which I am in prison—that I may make it clear, which is how I ought to speak. Walk in wisdom toward outsiders, making the best use of the time. Let your speech always be gracious, seasoned with salt, so that you may know how you ought to answer each person."

Paul is specifically asking God to open doors so he can share. He knows what he wants to share—Jesus. How he shares is driven by wisdom, grace, and respect. Even if someone doesn't agree with us, if we approach them boldly like that, they will listen, and we will probably gain a friend. As I think of it, I've yet to be rejected because of what I believed, and if I share it clearly, simply, lovingly, with respect, they listen.

SIX

LIVING OUR FAITH WITH ALL OUR FAITHS PRESENT

For God so loved the world, that he gave his only Son, that whoever believes in him should not perish but have eternal life.

—John 3:16

And do not fear those who kill the body but cannot kill the soul. Rather fear him who can destroy both soul and body in hell. . . . [E]ven the hairs of your head are all numbered. Fear not, therefore; you are of more value than many sparrows. So everyone who acknowledges me before men, I also will acknowledge before my Father who is in heaven, but whoever denies me before men, I also will deny before my Father who is in heaven.

—Matthew 10:28–33

Eboo Patel is the founder and executive director of the Interfaith Youth Core, an international nonprofit building the interfaith youth movement. An American Muslim, he writes extensively for publications like "The Faith Divide" blog, the *Washington Post,* the *Harvard Divinity School Bulletin,* the *Chicago Tribune,* and the *Sunday Times of India,* and speaks regularly on National Public Radio and many television programs. He lives in Chicago, Illinois.

A few years ago, I flew to Chicago to get to know him.

I had read his book, *Acts of Faith,* so I knew his story. As we drove from the airport to his office downtown, I told him my story candidly and honestly. How would this Chicago-born, Yankee, Indian-American respond to my story? I told him all of it, from growing up in East Texas, to discovering the biblical concept of the kingdom of God, to getting to know Vietnamese communists. I told him what I learned working in Afghanistan with Muslims, speaking at the World Islamic Forum, and then working in the West Bank, and what it was leading to in Dallas–Fort Worth. He didn't judge me, but he listened and seemed grateful that I would want to get to know him and his work. In fact, he loved my story and

identified with it at several points. He was also very honest with me about his faith, and how he saw the world
and the challenges we all face.

What really stood out was my visit with his staff. He
had several of them meet with me in a conference room.
Each began by telling his or her story. One was a young
Jewish woman who was rediscovering what it meant
to be a Jew. Another was of Middle-Eastern descent,
now an American who was a very devout and committed Muslim. These two talked about how they disagree
about what was going on in Gaza; they admitted that it
got tense between them sometimes, but that they still
worked together for peace.

The next person to speak was an Ivy League–educated
young man introduced as an evangelical. Evangelical
doesn't mean what it used to, so someone saying he is
evangelical doesn't necessarily mean what it did just
ten years ago. So I asked him about his denominational
background. He was Assembly of God, not a bastion of
leftward-leaning evangelicalism but very conservative. I
asked him several other questions and found out he really
was a conservative evangelical. I then asked him why he
worked with Eboo. He told me it was refreshing to be
able to be honest about what you believe and still work
together for the common good.

I asked all of them what it did to their faith, interacting

like that with believers from other religions. Did it make them question or become weaker in their faith? Every single one of them said it made their faith stronger.

This was the same experience I was having as I worked with people of other faiths. It didn't make me doubt my faith, though it did make me explore more deeply what I believe and why. It didn't weaken my faith; if anything it strengthened it.

This really hit me hard. I felt at home with these young adults. They were living out in a group what I had been living out as an individual. I later told my daughter, Jill, about these young people, and she said she had experienced the same thing growing up and traveling the world with me, working with the Vietnamese and other groups. As I look back, I felt I had sat at the table of the future, and it was very, very good.

As I flew back to Dallas, I realized that this interfaith concept was perhaps the biggest stumbling block to the very thing it wanted to prevent: religious conflict that spills over into everyday life. I don't like the term *interfaith*. It's the nebulous, fuzzy feeling; it's a we're-all-going-to-the-same-place-just-different-roads religion, a kind of Kumbaya experience. I don't know of a single imam who believes I can go to heaven rejecting the divinity of the prophet Mohammed's message. Neither do I know a single Bible-believing evangelical pastor who believes a person can go to heaven denying the divinity of Jesus or the exclusivity of the cross.

Still, I believe that our faiths must work together, and I believe Christians are called into relationships with people of other faiths. But if you don't call it *interfaith*, what do you call it?

The Difference a Word Makes

As I sat on the plane I was tinkering with what words to use to describe what I was seeing and experiencing. I wanted it to carry the idea that we all had unique faiths that we wouldn't compromise, but that we could still get together and get along. Then it hit me: *multifaith*. That's the word that describes what's happening with so many of us.

I researched the word and quickly saw that it was a word already in use. But I wanted to give it a certain shape and meaning in the context of what I saw God doing in our church and elsewhere. As I've thought about it more, I've realized multifaith has six dimensions. If we understand its full meaning, I believe it will help us as American Christians to grasp its potential for the church and for the world. Multifaith is the new platform on which we must relate. The interfaith platform wasn't made for conservative believers who took their faith literally and wanted to live according to their holy books.

Multifaith Is Perfect for Americans

In the first place, we need to recognize that multifaith really isn't anything new. It's how our country was set up. Among the freedoms we lift up, freedom of religion is right at the top. We created a country that decided to let people of different religions live together—a multifaith country.

America is a nation of immigrants, and over the decades, we've had to make space for everyone. At first that meant different expressions of Christianity; later it meant space for Jews and even the nonreligious and heretics. Today it means making room for Muslims. In a world where most countries either discriminate or even persecute minority religions, America offers a great gift: a model of how people of different faiths can live together without compromising our individual beliefs.

In November 2010 we held an event at Northwood called the Global Faith Forum (www.globalfaithforum .org). We prayed for two hundred but had about seven hundred from all faiths who came for the three-day event. People at the gathering were stunned that there was such candid, honest conversation on issues we disagree on but don't want to divide us in the public square. Our agenda for the program was built on the premise of multifaith—how we work in the world and how we can have relationships together. The seed of this book is in my two addresses that I gave at the event. We had Christians like Ray Bakke, Os Guinness, Mark Galli; we had the Vietnamese ambassador; we had capitalist and communist; we had clerics and world leaders—it was an incredible event. Os Guinness was interviewed by a reporter from Patheos, a website that engages the global dialogue about the world's religions and spirituality, on the Global Faith Forum at which he spoke:

> So many people think of the other religions either in terms of conflict or evangelism solely or interfaith dialogue. I think we have a vision here which is different. The idea of interfaith dialogue—that there's a lowest common denominator unity and if we talk long enough we'll all be able to agree—is wrong. Our differences are deep and irreducible. My own vision of a civil public square which is a political framework of rights, responsibilities and respect within which we're free to be faithful to our own faith and yet know how to engage with others peacefully, civilly, persuasively and so on. I know that's the vision here at Northwood, which is why I'm so delighted to cooperate because it's a relatively rare vision. Apologetics without self-righteousness.

Najeeba Syeed-Miller wrote an article called "Creating History in This Moment" for *Muslim Voices* and gave her reflections: "Rev. Roberts is a conservative, evangelical Christian. There are numerous topics upon which we most likely vehemently disagree. But there are places where we see eye to eye. He and I are both deeply rooted in our American identity and patriotic to our core.... We cannot just talk about Christians—we must step into the fray and engage as well. Rev. Roberts has extended an invitation and so what is your response to him?"

Multifaith Is Perfect for Religious Conservatives

I believe that the greatest challenge was not helping religious liberals to learn to get along. Religious liberals are famous for relativism in their faith so it doesn't seem all that different than the faith of others. Religious liberals tend to be much more open to the idea that people of all religions are going to heaven, that all religious roads eventually get there. So it's not hard for religious liberals to get along and to gather at interfaith gatherings.

The problem is that there are hardly any religious liberals in the world, though they often tend to be the intellectuals and so make the news. By far and away, the world is made up of devout, ardent religious conservatives, who believe everyone is going to hell except those who believe in their religion. These are the people who need to be reached if we're going to have a more peaceful world.

And these are the very people for whom multifaith was made. The person who is most passionate isn't going to compromise for the sake of unity. This is why most conservative Christians never sit down at interfaith gatherings. Religious conservatives don't believe one religion is as good as another. If a religious conservative were to discover that another religion had more truth, he or she would adopt it. The basis of faith for the religious conservative is what the Bible says, or what the Quran says, or what his holy book says. Multifaith is not about syncretism! If you google the word, you'll find some definitions that say it's about feeling an affinity with more than one religion, philosophy, or worldview. That's not what I believe, and neither is it what people of other faiths believe when we come together.

Multifaith not only respects but encourages religious people to say exactly what they believe, no matter how stark the differences. But it encourages them to do so in the spirit of peace.

Multifaith Is for Common Good

Multifaith works for the common good. We have to be honest and admit that when faith has interacted in the past, it has often led to persecution, wars, and conflict. In multifaith, we want to do better. We of different faiths should come together not so that we can change each other or agree on everything; instead our focus should be blessing our community and serving others. The best of the Christian faith teaches us that we should get along with people of other faiths and with people of no faith. As the New Testament says, "If possible, so far as it depends on you, live peaceably with all" (Romans 12:18).

Multifaith moves beyond tolerance and respect to action and collaboration to serve the good of the city and of your neighborhood. It will require learning; it will involve making mistakes; a lot of grace will need to be shown; time and again it will feel like you're starting all over again.

When I was in Saudi Arabia, one scholar said that he didn't hear me talk a lot about tolerance. I told him, maybe he was right. But I didn't just want to tolerate him. I said I wanted to be his friend, and to be friends with others.

Multifaith Is Honest

Sincere faith will not be able to use politically correct language. Truth is not tied to popular opinion. I want people to know what I believe, and I want to know honestly what they believe. There can be no trust, no relationship, not even a conversation, without honesty.

By multifaith I mean there are multiple faiths, and we can work together in respect. Researcher Ed Stetzer, who spoke at our Global Faith Forum, expressed it well in a blog he wrote for me. This later appeared in an article he wrote for *Christianity Today* in April 2011:

> Five years ago, I found myself sitting in an interfaith meeting. Gracious people from different religions and denominations had gathered together to plan for common research on congregations. We met at the Evangelical Lutheran Church of America headquarters in Chicago to plan the ongoing work of congregational research, a project launched and funded by a major grant through a charitable endowment. The goal of the Cooperative Congregational Studies Partnership was to bring together participants from Protestant, Catholic, Jewish, Muslim, Baha'i' and Orthodox churches to research and compare the realities of our work.
>
> I was one of those participants but was unsure if I belonged. During one of the main sessions, the facilitator explained that this research should lead to cooperative resourcing to help all our respective con-gregations. He suggested that we could jointly create, publish, and distribute resources to help congregations

deal with faith development, growth, and other issues.

At the appropriate time, and with my best smile, I raised my hand and said something like, "I am here for the research. I appreciate the funding that allows us to survey our churches, and I think it is helpful to use similar questions and metrics for better research. But I am not here to form a partnership to help one another and our congregations. I want to help the churches I serve, but part of the reason they exist is to convert some of you."

I paused, smiled, and worked hard not to sound menacing. Some of them looked at me as if I had just used a string of profanities. But others nodded in agreement. And then the Muslim Imam seated next to me spoke up and said, "I actually feel the same way."

Though we were in a minority in that group of (predominantly) liberal Protestants, we represented the growing groups. We believed in sharing and growing our faith, we did not think that we were all worshiping the same God or gods, and we were not there to pretend we believed the same things. In other words, our goal was not a merging of faiths, a blurring of belief, or even interfaith partnership.

Multifaith not only encourages but requires that type of honesty with one another.

Multifaith Creates Lasting Relationships

A couple of years ago, I spoke at the Swiss Foreign Ministry on "Religion and Conflict Transformation" to five hundred world leaders. Later that week, I flew to London, where over sixty thousand Muslims were gathered; I spoke there in a room where Islamic world leaders and others were gathered. Each time, I would be introduced as an "evangelical pastor," and trust me when I say you could feel the air in the room sucked right out.

After each talk, several people said to me, "When you were introduced as an evangelical, and then you explained what that meant and what you believed, I thought, *Yuck!*" That's understandable, because to outsiders the word *evangelical* has become a dirty word. It means arrogant, bullying, bigoted, colonial, judgmental, loving Jews but not Arabs and Muslims, and so forth. Then that comment would be followed up by, "But when I began to listen to you, it made sense, and I understood it. I didn't know there were evangelicals like you. You've made me rethink my view."

As I told one group with several imams present, "Because I have rejected Mohammed as a divine prophet, I cannot go to heaven. Any imam and most Muslims would tell you that. But it doesn't mean they're bigoted or evil. It means they value the truth of their Quran. In the same way, I cannot reject my Bible and what it teaches." All the imams were grinning and nodding their heads in agreement. Something fantastic was taking place in that room. There was no need for anyone to get angry, upset, emotional, or hateful. We were there as friends and fellow global citizens trying to understand each other and how to get along. The freedom to be honest helped us appreciate one another and begin to form friendships in ways we couldn't have before.

Multifaith Deepens Our Faith

When I once visited Syria for a conference, I became fast friends with an imam who had studied at the Harvard of Islam, the Al Aqsa Institute in Cairo. He told me that because he knew I was coming to visit, he had attended a Baptist church in Syria; he wanted to understand me more. He said while he was there, he prayed, because he wanted to identify with the people. Three times each day, during the conference, this imam would gather the Muslims, and they would line up and pray in the center while the rest of us would visit quietly.

I watched them do it a few times, and thought to myself, *I'd like to be over there praying with them.* I love to pray. Daily worship and prayer are a deep part of my everyday life. I'd prayed with Muslims in the deserts of Afghanistan as they would lay out their carpets; I'd take a knee behind them and pray in my way, while they prayed in theirs. But this was a conference; there were several people there. How would they respond if I asked to pray with them? It's one thing to be with friends in a desert where few people will see you. I thought of how this imam had gone out of his way to respect me. So one time when they headed over to pray, I asked if I could pray with them. I said I'd pray quietly, and that I would be praying in the name of Jesus, and if he didn't want me to, I'd understand.

He quickly said, "Yes, we would love you to pray with us."

I stood between a young engineer named Ghaith and an American Muslim, Suhail Khan; both of these men I consider friends. I told them to tell me what to do and when. I felt like I was back in the Catholic church with my grandmother, trying to figure out when to kneel and when to stand up straight. I have a bum knee that won't bend very well, so I did the best I could.

When I prayed, I prayed for them by name in my heart. I asked God to give them the revelation of Jesus, just like he had given me and millions of others throughout history. I asked Jesus to let them know that I love them deeply and would serve them any way possible.

Afterward my friend Ghaith said, "Bob, I care about you. I want you in heaven with us."

I told him, "I feel the exact same way. Only God can reveal himself to us and cause us to see."

I asked them if I could pray for them in my tradition. They said yes. So I got us in a circle, I laid my hands on each of them briefly, and prayed a prayer of reconciliation, hope, and that the divine presence of Jesus would flood them, protect them, and be near them.

Did I sense the presence of God? Yes, I sensed it powerfully! How could I pray with Muslims and feel that? I pray every week with Christians who are cheats, adulterers, thieves, mean, gossips, two-faced . . . If I can pray with them and feel God's presence, then I reckon a Muslim or Jew won't hurt a lot when I'm praying.

My worship is focused on God and not those I stand near. In my early days of walking with Jesus, my worship was tied to the music and those around me. But in time, I began to realize my worship was not an emotional experience based on the presence of others but a profound realization of the presence of Jesus. If I bow to another god, that's one thing. But if I bow to God made flesh in Jesus, all is well.

God is everywhere, and his temple is also in my heart. If that's the case, I can worship anywhere. If that's the case, all of life is worship. If that's the case, for me multifaith is one of the most exciting ideas, because it means I am at worship when I am serving and reaching out and even praying with those who don't believe in Jesus. In Psalm 139, David says, "If I make my bed in Sheol you are there!" (v. 8). Jesus worshipped wherever he was—with the Twelve, with the three, with the masses, and alone.

Twenty years ago I might have felt uncomfortable worshipping with people of different faiths. Not anymore. And that's because I have come to believe worship is highly evangelistic. Fellow Christians have told me they sensed God the most and worshipped him most powerfully when they have prayed or worshipped with people who don't know Jesus. It makes perfect sense: Jesus is being proclaimed, even if only by us in silent prayer!

Maria's Story

I've had to use my own experience a lot in this book, but my experience is pretty typical of those who get involved in multifaith events. So listen to what one of our members, Maria Escamilla, wrote after our Multifaith Weekend.

When Northwood Church announced the Multifaith Weekend, I jumped at the chance to sign up, knowing this was a unique opportunity for my family to visit a synagogue, mosque, and church all in one weekend.

As you will recall, the multifaith event was held at a Jewish synagogue on Friday, an Islamic mosque on Saturday, and at Northwood Church on Sunday.

> My personal reason for participating was to learn more about Judaism and Islam from the people themselves. I'm currently involved in supporting missionary work and hope to increase my involvement in the coming years. Knowledge and appreciation of other cultures and beliefs is essential. It was very interesting to observe the different worship services as a guest in a respectful environment. And of course as a Christian I also believe it's good that all people have an opportunity to hear God's Word as they did on Sunday.

Maria clearly saw this as both an educational event and the opportunity for those of other faiths to hear a distinctly Christian message. But what about involving her children?

> They were both really interested in the whole weekend, the thirteen-year-old more so. The seven-year-old got a little bored at times. But both asked questions throughout as to what was going on during the different services. As a family we enjoy cultural events and learning about different cultures around the

world. All three of us are preparing for future mission trips to serve those in need, so they really enjoyed the Multifaith Weekend.

It was surprising to hear that even the youngest girl is preparing for "future mission trips." This seems quite ambitious; however, it's no surprise that she would want to go wherever her mom and older sister are going, and in general, children are easily influenced by those around them. This can be good or bad.

At first at the mosque, the seven-year-old didn't want to wear a headscarf, but when she saw many others with headscarves, she wanted one too. A Muslim lady gave her own headscarf to keep. The girls tried some of the ethnic foods the Muslim ladies prepared and were surprised at how spicy one of the curried potato pies [was]—it was really hot, but good.

The girls were also surprised to see that the Jewish book for the Shabbat was opposite . . . since Hebrew is read from right to left. They enjoyed trying to follow along.

As Christians, the roots of our faith are in Judaism, and if we ever want to really understand our Bibles, we should study Hebrew, the original language of the Old Testament.

> We loved how reverent and respectful the Jewish and Muslim people are in their places of worship. It appears none would show disrespect in their worship sloppily dressed. We thought that was a good lesson and example to emulate.

This last observation is a strikingly embarrassing one. As a Christian, it seems sad that somehow those of other religious faiths have a better grasp of the need to show reverence to God than we do.

So how did things go on Sunday at the Christian church?

> During the service at Northwood on Sunday, Pastor Roberts asked if the participants would be willing to continue getting to know each other so we could serve the community. It appeared that many agreed they would like to do that. Pastor Roberts hoped we could meet while respecting our fundamentally different beliefs and I believe this was achieved.

Didn't she wonder or worry about this combination of different faiths?

I can see how people can have a negative reaction to this. When I first saw the promotions for the Multifaith Weekend, a red flag went off in my mind. I had to make sure this wasn't an "all paths lead to God" event. It wasn't at all, but I can see where people might think that. God commands us to love one another. On a local level, we got the opportunity to make acquaintance with our neighbors, so we can get to know them and better serve their needs.

That's what I'm talking about! This is as bold as love can get!

SEVEN

CHALLENGING ALL MY TRIBE

Behold, I have set before you an open door, which no one is able to shut. I know that you have but little power, and yet you have kept my word and have not denied my name. . . . Behold, I stand at the door and knock. If anyone hears my voice and opens the door, I will come in to him and eat with him, and he with me.

—**Revelation 3:8, 20**

A couple of years ago, I took a group of young pastors to Georgetown University in Washington DC to a conference I was speaking at called "Common Word." I wanted these young pastors and leaders to meet Muslim clerics and leaders, as well as other people in the DC area I'd come to know through my multifaith work—people from the Vietnamese Embassy, from our State Department, from the Islamic Society of North America (ISNA), and more.

Sayeed Sayid is an early organizer of ISNA and one of its leaders, so I wanted them to meet him. He's one of the kindest men I've ever met. We met him in his office, which is on the third floor of the United Methodist Building next door to the Supreme Court. When the small talk was over, he began to tell his story.

He came to America to give his family an opportunity. Much of what is thought to represent Islam around the world is usually more about specific cultures than Islam itself. He said Americans would often ask why he didn't go live in some country in the Middle East, since he was Muslim. He would tell them he wanted to be in America, where there was religious freedom and opportunity.

Sayid also talked about how people would try to convert him without really understanding him. One year, he said, "The Southern Baptists sent out a brochure to pray for all Muslims to be converted. They should especially witness to us during Ramadan, when we fast, because we would be so hungry!"

As I was leaving, he thanked me for bringing the pastors. Then he said, "Do you know what your name means in Arabic?" I didn't. He told me: "Door."

He also said, "That's what you are, Bob, a door to connect our people."

He didn't know that one of the promise verses God had given me in my ministry was that of the open door. That particular year, without sharing it with people, both Christians and Muslims alike would talk about me being a door. A verse that means a lot to me (one that Eddy Leo from Abba Love Church in Indonesia taught on at our church) is from Colossians 4:2–6:

Continue steadfastly in prayer, being watchful in it with thanksgiving. At the same time, pray also for us, *that God may open to us a door for the word*, to declare the mystery of Christ, on account of which I am in prison—that I may make it clear, which is how I ought to speak. Walk in wisdom toward outsiders, making the best use of the time. Let your speech always be gracious, seasoned with salt, so that you may know how you ought to answer each person. (Emphasis mine.)

I used to think the greatest thing I could do was connect the church and believers globally. I still think that is a great thing. But I now believe the greatest thing I can do is connect people not just religiously but civilly, humanly, and socially. I want to connect the world and people of faith to serve the greater sphere of humanity, to sweat together as we work for the common good, and to talk to one another about our faiths. And as God wills, I want to be a doorway for them to meet Jesus.

Tribalism

But it is not easy to live out our faith consistently. One of the things that gets in the way is our tribalism. We just naturally form ourselves into groups—families, cultures, affinity or interest groups—and then we identify with them.

We are born into families, and this is where we get our values and some security and provision. A single family cannot be self-sufficient, so clans came into being, and people lived in compounds made up of extended family for more protection and more provision. Clans were limited to a location, but a tribe could spread out across an expanse of land. Tribes brought security and protection and also a lot of culture. Music, food, art, values, rituals, faith—all of these were determined by the tribe.

But because of human sin, tribes also bring with them negative things. Snobbery; elitism; racism; religious bigotry; the desire to conquer other tribes. Unfortunately, even among religious tribes, there can be a desire to conquer other religions, as history has shown.

Recently, I was with a leading ayatollah from Iran. He kept asking me about evangelicals and why they were so involved in politics; why did they want control? I told him because we all want to be ayatollahs! He laughed, because he recognized how common it is even for religious tribes to want to conquer.

One way tribalism raises its ugly head today is when we see Christians vilifying people of other faiths. When we hosted the Building Bridges event, we were told that some people were saying the Muslims were coming to pray with us only so they could take over our church. When we become tribal, these are the sorts of things we say. When pastors and other followers of Jesus begin to relate to people of other faiths, I tell them, "Never, never, never vilify another religion. Instead, exalt Jesus, lift him up. You don't have to trash another religion to promote Jesus."

This is crucial. Everything is in the public square; we

must realize that whatever we blog or tweet, the whole world sees. How do we want to speak of Jesus? Often because of how we say some things and vilify others, people don't hear the gospel of Jesus Christ because they can't get past our hate. We have to speak with what I call "one conversation"—not one conversation for just us Christians and another conversation for our public face, but a single conversation so that we are consistent, clear, and considerate in what we say.

People see and judge us by our tribe, and we see other people in the context of their tribes. That's fine up to a point. Labels help us locate people within their culture and setting. But too often tribes begin to divide us and make us suspicious of one another. This happens even in our religious tribes.

One blog I especially like is by Micah Fries. Recently he posted some comments about his efforts to transcend the tribalism of his church. It began like this:

> One of the most fascinating, and disappointing, things I have seen from the church in quite some time is the incredible anti-Muslim sentiment coming from our Christian ranks, particularly since 9/11. Now, don't misunderstand me, I believe in the exclusivity of Jesus. I am convinced that John 14:6 ["I am the way, and the truth, and the life"] is accurate, and that our

faith in Jesus Christ alone provides salvation. I am in no way trying to minimize the very real differences that exist between Christianity and Islam.

At the same time, however, I am convinced that our faith requires of us humility towards God and man; it requires of us that we love all people, and view all humanity as people with incredible value. With that in mind it is concerning to me that so many Christians seem to view Muslims as if they were the enemy. Ephesians 6:12 reminds us that humanity is not our enemy. Our struggle is not against each other.

Jesus, of course, came to transcend tribalism. Jesus was the end of tribes—his was a kingdom, and he is the King. There were twelve tribes that made up the nation of Israel, and even then, people became more tribal in parties like the Pharisees or Sadducees. The gospel is about crossing tribes; when we make it tribal, we slow it, distort it, and limit it. This is why Jesus loved Gentiles, drunks, prostitutes, and so forth, even when his tribe despised them.

That's why Micah Fries went on to say:

Even if Muslims were our enemy, Scripture is abundantly clear that our call is to love our enemies, and to pray for them. Regardless, then, of whether you view

Muslims as your enemy or not, it would be a denial of the practice of our faith to treat them poorly, to fail in any attempt to be gracious to them and to live out the call of Jesus Christ to love them. I am committed to living out the Gospel, as I share it with all people, and I am convinced that few will respond to our gospel message if we are combative and attacking, [but] many may be interested if we humbly share the truth of the Gospel in love, within the context of relationship.

Listen—Don't Fix

I've discovered some simple, practical ways to begin to transcend my natural tribalism—like listening more than I talk.

We are quick to tell others what we believe and why we are right, and how they need to change their beliefs. I'm from Texas, and we like fixin' everything. But we have to resist that temptation. Instead of judging where people are and what they believe, I've found it better to ask questions and listen to them talk about their lives, their families, their dreams, their disappointments.

I remember one time talking to a man who has been called the brain of Hezbollah. We wound up speaking about religion, and he said he believes, more than anything, religion is about mercy. That surprised me, coming from him. But I was pleased, because I agree with him. I would have never guessed he believed that if I hadn't spent a lot of time in conversation with him, listening to him.

When I listen to other tribes, I begin to better understand them as fellow human beings, with similar feelings, struggles, griefs, and joys. When I was with a particular group in Gaza, I had many preconceived ideas about who they were, so I was surprised to learn many of these men had earned PhDs in the West. They were deliberate in what they said. They were gracious. They each had a story of losing loved ones. They spoke of their dreams of the future. As a result, I've learned as much as God loves the Jews, he loves the Palestinians just as much. I once heard a friend say the reason that the Jews and Palestinians can't reconcile is because they are wounded and victimized tribes who can't let go. The Jews were victimized by the Germans and Europeans and say "never again"; they now have a homeland and will do whatever it takes to make it secure. The Palestinians have been victimized by the Jews, who drove them out of their land and made them people without a country, many having lost their homes and livelihood. Now I have empathy for both groups.

This is the sort of thing listening can do for us.

Again, read of Micah Fries's experience, when he realized how much hostility Christians had toward Muslims
in his area:

> With this in mind [that Christ calls us to love everyone],
> I began a while ago to try and connect with some in our
> Muslim community here in St. Joseph. I have visited the
> local Mosque on a couple of occasions for their Friday
> prayer service, and we have enjoyed the presence of at
> least one of my Muslim friends at our worship service
> as well here at Frederick. . . . While there is certainly
> much we can learn from others who have studied vari-
> ous faiths, I have been surprised at just how much I have
> learned by studying from those who are immersed in
> the faith itself. . . . I have gladly given them the freedom
> to share with me what they believe about Islam. In fact,
> it has been eye opening to learn about their faith from
> someone practicing that faith.

Witness—Don't Manipulate

It helps me listen and love people of other faiths if I
see myself first and foremost as a witness of what God
has done and will do in Christ. God does not hold me
accountable for what other tribes do; he does hold me
accountable for how I lead my tribe and whether I am

a voice for good or evil. Tribes function best when they support identity, values, culture, and belonging, not when they act like gangs or the police or the mafia. When we act like that, we're acting out of fear, trying to control others by law and physical or psychological violence. When I understand myself as a witness of what God is doing, I don't have to make things happen. I am free to love and witness to his love.

We have to keep reminding ourselves that evangelism is really not up to us. Our job is to proclaim and live the gospel, loving God and others. I've met people from other religions who became Christians, and often it was not because someone explained everything to them. I recently visited with a man who told me, "Jesus appeared to me in a dream, like a vision, and told me to follow him—and I did." This man is an exceptional artist and painter, and I asked him to paint a picture of the Jesus who appeared to him. He did, and Jesus looks Middle Eastern. I guess he would! "I had to find someone to help understand who Jesus was," he told me. "It was Jesus revealing himself to me that made me follow him." We have a saying at Northwood, "Serve not to convert; serve because you are converted." Theologically that's true on two fronts: first, it is God who draws men to himself, and second, it is the work of the Spirit that convicts and draws men to Jesus.

The same is true with all of us, even when it's not as dramatic as a dream. At the end of the day, evangelism is merely telling others who God is, and it is the Spirit who quickens and the Son who reveals himself so people can choose to follow him.

This is how Micah Fries approached the Muslims in his community. He said that because he approached them humbly, listening first, "They have given me the freedom to clearly share what I believe to be true about Christianity."

Critique your own faith before you critique someone else's faith.

I no longer buy books on Islam or other religions from Christian bookstores. Often there is the attempt to win arguments—so the result is confusion over what is true and what is not. You can read firsthand sources. I've listened to young Arabs criticize themselves. I think it's healthy and a good lesson for all of us. At the conference in Doha, many of the revolutionaries of the Arab Spring came to speak; these were primarily young people. They were from Egypt, Tunisia, Libya, and other places. I got to eat meals with them and talk to them. Some of us exchanged Twitter addresses and have kept in touch since. But there was a split between the older Islamists there and the younger people; there were passionate discussions (some might say arguments). Sometimes, the greatest witnessing we can do is to our own tribe, to remind them how God loves us and how he loves others and that Jesus is for all people, not just those in our tribe. Jesus said, "Other sheep have I." He meant it.

The only tribe you can change is your tribe.

How am I stopping various forms of fear-based behavior within my own tribe? I thought the greatest thing I could do to bring down tension between Christians and Muslims was for *me* to befriend Muslims. That's not true. The greatest thing I can do is lead a congregation and churches to connect with Muslims *so they can see for themselves.* I won't change everyone in my tribe, but some will change and they will lead the charge. Jesus made his twelve disciples his primary mission, with specific instructions to them to make the message global—crossing all tribes and nations. When Christian tribes try to isolate themselves, they deny the very thing Jesus commanded them to do.

Live your faith to the best of your ability.

You represent far more than your tribe: if you follow Jesus, *you represent him.* If observers don't respect the way you live for Jesus, why will they want to follow him? When people look at you, what impression are you giving of Jesus?

Take Courage—Do Not Fear

I heard former US Ambassador to Israel Feldman say, "There are fleeting moments of opportunity that most don't recognize, and when they do it's too late. But most, when they see them, they don't have the courage to act."[1] In light of that, I crafted a new definition of leadership: seeing and recognizing unique moments of opportunity, then seizing them with boldness and courage.

Courage is the ability to move forward in confidence knowing you are doing the right thing regardless of what is taking place around you. I've been to many crazy places in the world, but I always come back to Jesus's two words, which are all over the Bible: "Fear not."

Real courage also means loving people others despise. I have a friend who spends time with a world leader most Americans love to hate. That leader needs God, and maybe my friend can help him find God. My friend may even get in trouble for being with this man; that's why I love my friend. He is being like Jesus, who took a Simon and turned him into Peter, and took a Saul and turned him into Paul. I told Southern Baptists at a recent pastors conference that the greatest thing they could do for the gospel was to love a Muslim, the very people many Christians "love to hate." If we did that, maybe our missionaries to Muslims in other parts of the world would be given grace in their context. If we love the ones we think are the hardest to love, then we really can love everyone. Just maybe, if we treat even "hard" people with respect and show love, as Jesus did, it just might, at a minimum, prevent a war.

Two Billion Doors

A while ago, I was invited by Al Jazeera to participate in a conference in Doha with the think tank called NYON, of which I'm a part. One evening we had a chance to go to the Suk, or Arab market, and I saw people getting their names printed in Arabic on jewelry. I asked one jeweler if it is true that Bob in Arabic means *door*, and he said yes. I have a little St. Christopher medal, so I showed it to him and asked if he could make a pendant of an ancient door and engrave my name in Arabic on the door, along with Revelation 3:8 ("Behold, I have set before you an open door, which no one is able to shut"). He said he could do it, and I could have it in two days.

When I went back to pick it up, I couldn't believe what I saw. It wasn't little; it was a huge silver "bling" that only a rap singer could love! The door pendant was not ancient as I had seen, but looked like a common door. I have never worn it—it's just not me. But I thanked him, paid him, and laugh every time I look at it. I keep it in my study at my house to remind me that I'm always to be a door.

But what if each follower of Jesus were a door—that's two billion doors! I hate to admit this, but I've learned I have far more to fear from my own tribe than I do from another tribe. If you are going to be bold as love, you'd better get ready for your own tribe to give you more headaches than the tribe you want to connect with. At worst, the other tribe could kill you—and that isn't likely. Your own tribe can make your entire life miserable . . . if you let them. Don't! Jesus hung out with drunks, whores, tax collectors, cheats—and his own tribe hated him for it. Are you in trouble with your own tribe?

EIGHT

FORGIVING WITH ALL MY HEART

*For he himself is our peace, who has made us both one and
has broken down in his flesh the dividing wall of hostility by
abolishing the law of commandments expressed in ordinances,
that he might create in himself one new man in place of the
two, so making peace, and might reconcile us both to God in
one body through the cross, thereby killing the hostility.*

—Ephesians 2:14–16

*. . . and forgive us our debts, as we also have forgiven our
debtors. And lead us not into temptation, but deliver us from
evil. For if you forgive others their trespasses, your heavenly
Father will also forgive you, but if you do not forgive others their
trespasses, neither will your Father forgive your trespasses.*

—Matthew 6:12–15

I remember when our church began to pray about a city overseas to work in, a man who had accepted Christ in our church suggested we consider a city in Vietnam. My "preacher's" response was, "Let's just pray about it."

He picked up on my reluctance and asked, "You weren't in the war; why do you feel this way?"

I knew why. My father had pastored near Shepherd Air Force Base in Wichita Falls, Texas. Every Sunday a group of young air force men worshipped with us. Afterward, every Sunday afternoon, my mom would set up a special table, and all these soldiers would come and eat with us. They taught me and my brother how to shine our shoes, and we admired them. They told us what boot camp was like and when they would ship out. We would get cards from them and hear from them. But some of them didn't make it back, and that had a profound impact on how I viewed Vietnam and the Vietnamese.

Something had to happen in me if we were ever going to go to Vietnam.

The Heart of Faith

A number of questions have driven my walk with God and my ministry. The first is, "When will Jesus be enough?" This question took me to the Sermon on the Mount and the kingdom of God and what it meant to love Jesus, live for him, and be transformed by him personally, in all areas of my life.

A second question is, "What if the church is the missionary?" This question led me to think about what it would look like if the body of Christ were released upon the grid of society to serve humanity in all the domains in which people normally work. What would it be like if our whole church was transformed by Jesus to reach out to others?

Another question I've asked a lot is, "What would it look like for the modern church to turn the world upside down in a healthy way?" To me, the answer to that question—and really the other two questions as well—begins with forgiveness, the core message of Jesus. It's what Jesus did on the cross for us that allows us to have a relationship with God. It's what Jesus has commanded us to do with others to have a relationship with him and others.

Forgiveness is the absolute hardest thing to do, but it is the most vital thing we can do to be healthy, whole, fulfilled, and most importantly, connected to God. One of my favorite writers is Miroslav Volf, an ethnic Croatian. He had finished his doctoral dissertation—on forgiveness—and was defending it, when his doctoral supervisor Jürgen Moltmann asked him, "Can you embrace a Checkni [Serbian fighter of Croatia during WWII and the war in the 90s]?" Volf's response: "I can't, but as a follower of Christ I should be able to."[1] That led to his book *Exclusion and Embrace.*

Someone has to be the first to stretch out his hand to forgive the other and to ask for forgiveness. When a young couple is fighting and they come in for me to counsel them, there's always enough blame to go around for everyone. I often ask, "Who wants to be the person to begin the forgiving process?"

When it comes to our relationship with Muslims, we must, as followers of Jesus, forgive Muslims for the way they have mistreated Christians through the ages (and even today). We must also be the first to say, "Forgive us for not loving you like Jesus loves you."

Never kill in the name of God—if anything, we should lose our lives. Ours is a faith that martyrs have given their lives for, allowing others to kill them because they refuse to deny Christ and his kingdom. This is bold love.

From Fear to Gratitude

One of the great joys I had recently was getting to know Kevin Kelly, technology expert, author, and founder of *Wired* magazine. He's his own kind of person. He is not only an engineer but a philosopher as well. He told me how he became a Christian.

He had been in Iran as a photographer in 1980 and had to leave suddenly. The only place he could fly to was Jerusalem, and he wound up with a room at the YMCA. He went out to see the old city, and ended up at the Church of the Holy Sepulchre. He stayed there so long, it was too late to return to the YMCA; they don't let people in after a certain hour. So he returned to the church and spent the night there.

That night, he had a strong sense that he should follow Jesus. Something told him to go home and be ready to die by October 31. So he went home, bought a bike, and started bicycling from the West Coast to the East Coast of the United States. He stopped along the way to reconnect with his relatives and friends, to make sure that he was right with everyone. If there were anything wrong, he asked forgiveness. He was preparing for his death.

He made it to the East Coast by October 30. He went to bed that night, expecting not to wake up the next morning. He had trouble sleeping, and he began to think about what the voice in Jerusalem had said to him. That voice hadn't told him he would die, but to be ready to die.

It was the traveling and the preparing for his death, he said, that led him to his rebirth. It was at the end of that trip that he really began to live.

His Christmas card to his family in 2007 said this:

All of us begin in the same place. Whether purified or not, we are not owed our life. Our existence is an unnecessary extravagance, a wild gesture, an unearned gift. Not just at birth. The eternal surprise is being funneled to us daily, hourly, minute by minute, every second. Yet, we are terrible recipients. We are no good at being helpless, humble, or indebted. Being needy is not celebrated on daytime TV shows, or in self-help books. We make lousy kindees.

I've slowly changed my mind about spiritual faith. I once thought it was chiefly about believing in an unmeasurable reality, that it had a lot in common with hope. But after many years of examining the lives of the people whose spiritual character I most respect, I've come to see that their faith rests on gratitude, rather than hope. They exude a sense of being indebted, and a state of being thankful. When the truly faithful worry, it's not about doubt (which they have), but it's about how they might not maximize the tremendous gift given them. How they might be ungrateful. The faithful I admire are not certain about much except this: that this state of being embodied, inflated with life, brimming with possibilities, is so over-the-top unlikely, so extravagant, so unconditional, so far out beyond physical entropy, that is it indistinguishable from love. And most amazing of all, like my hitchhiking rides, this love-gift is an extravagant gesture you can count on. No matter how bad the weather, soiled the past, broken the heart, hellish the war—all that is behind the universe is conspiring to help you—if you will let it.

Kevin is a kind, gentle, and very grateful man. His spirit is the kind of spirit we need more of. I like what he said about hope versus gratitude. It's true. Those who live by hope need, want, expect something to get fixed or righted—and there's nothing wrong with that. We all feel that. But gratitude asks *what I am doing with this gift of life God has given me?*

From Complaint to Mercy

I was with a Palestinian leader in the West Bank. I asked him what he thought of the two-state solution. He told me it wouldn't work. I asked why. He said, "Because at the core you have two cultures that live by victim mentality." He said both Jews and Palestinians feel like the victim. "Until someone has the courage to forgive and start afresh with grace, nothing can change."

Some people say, "No justice, no peace." It sounds right, but it's not quite right. After one talk, a man asked me, "Do you believe there can be peace without justice?" I told him: "No justice, no peace. But the truth is there will never be enough justice to satisfy all the pain and hurt in this world. If we don't forgive, and move forward, we will forever be trying to balance an impossible scorecard."

The man who asked the question didn't like the answer, but Gandhi's grandson, who was sitting beside me at the time, grinned; he liked it! My response was a Gandhi quote!

I was in Istanbul with a man many consider a terrorist. He said to me, "In Islam, it's the idea that my mercy expands, extends to everything. Either a man lives by mercy, or he lives by fear. There are five ideas taken from the five pillars of Islam. Mercy is the key to all of them."

I told him I agreed with him in some ways. For the Christian, that's what the cross is all about.

He also said, "Religion must serve people, and not

people serve religion, or it gets very dangerous. God doesn't need someone to serve him; he is so rich in everything."

I asked him, "Why don't you let me bring a group of pastors to meet with you and your friends in your country, and let's put that mercy thing to work between us."

He said, "If you think they will come."

Today the world experiences as much tension as ever. But this is also a time of great opportunity to reach out to the other side. Everyone knows that things are broken, and something radical and something different has to be tried, or we may wind up starting World War III.

Taking the First Step

That something radical is this: Someone has to be the first to reach out to the other side to build the relationship. Someone has to take the first step. Someone has to be willing to risk rejection. We have to stop waiting for someone to meet us halfway or we may die waiting.

So many things could be written about forgiveness. So many things have to be forgiven. Life cannot be managed without forgiveness—it's simply impossible. Jesus knew that. When Jesus suggested that a Jew carry a Roman soldier's backpack for two miles (Matthew 5), it was beyond comprehension in that day.

All forgiveness bears the usual hallmarks. Someone

has been wronged, and at that point that person has a choice to be filled with anger or mercy.

Recently the news featured a story about a ninety-two-year-old American who had kept a Japanese flag he had found in the helmet of a Japanese soldier. It was signed by Japanese families who had sent their sons to war. This man wanted to give the flag back before he died. So some men from the Japanese embassy came to retrieve the flag; he shook hands with them and said, "We aren't enemies anymore."

In this case, there were sixty-seven years of time that helped bring healing. But we don't always have sixty-seven years for things to heal. Unless someone reaches out, things can escalate and get wildly out of control.

As I said, there are two paths. The normal human path is to stay angry, and this leads to bitterness and hate. People who give in to anger live for revenge; they are not satisfied until the score is evened. But even after the score is evened, they are left with all the negative emotions that have taken hold of their heart.

The Jesus path is, when the offense happens, to express mercy and forgiveness, which leads to relationship and reconciliation. It doesn't mean the hurt was right or didn't matter. It only means forgiveness is going to define how we respond. Desmund Tutu, who led the Peace and Reconciliation hearings in South Africa after apartheid, often said, "There is no future without forgiveness."

Fast forward from my conversation with the man who suggested our church work in Vietnam. I was going to serve the people from the country whose soldiers had killed people I looked up to, and I didn't like it. I knew well we'd lost fifty-eight thousand troops there. I didn't know the Vietnamese death count was between two and three million casualties. I remember the first time I went to Vietnam, the plane couldn't pull into the terminal, and it took a while to open the door. I was tired, had flown all day and night to get there, and it was hot and humid. No one was that friendly, and neither was I.

Finally the door was opened, and in came a couple of Vietnamese soldiers; they walked down the aisle looking at everyone. I didn't like them. I looked out the window and realized on the very tarmac on which I was sitting, bodies of American soldiers had been stacked to be flown back to the United States.

So I can't tell you that my anger went away fast—it didn't. It took one relationship at a time and a few years of engaging with the Vietnamese to see it in a totally different light. As I got to know the Vietnamese, I learned it's a matter of perspective. The Chinese had been there a thousand years, the French two hundred fifty years, and the Americans barely fifteen years—a blip! If people who don't acknowledge Jesus can forgive and move forward, what does it say about me, someone who knows him, but doesn't forgive?

Sadly, it is often pastors and other religious leaders who hate the most and are the quickest to condemn people who don't follow their religion. I believe pastors, more than anyone else, have a unique role to play. The power of a pastor is not having a "brainalogue" with a global faith leader of another religion; that's nice, but it changes only two people. Instead, it's to connect congregations in people-to-people relationships. Even though this book is about not fearing, many pastors still do. Generally, they fear not knowing what to do—and it's easier to do nothing and keep people happy than to risk bold love and get beat up.

There are three things that we pastors must do if we want to be a force for peace in our communities and the world. First, we must interpret. Where is the world going? What does it mean? What has God called us to in this time? Second, we must model. We cannot merely shame people or challenge them; we must build our own relationships so others can see what it looks like. Third, we must facilitate. Here's the good news: our preaching is stronger, more clear, because we are exposing our people to new people and new ideas.

But . . . they're already exposed, because we live in diverse communities that are becoming more so. Now, though, we are exposing them through the filter of church. By interpreting, modeling, and facilitating exposure, our focus becomes deliberate and proactive. Instead of watching young people leave our churches because we don't answer the questions, instead of members asking what they should do with their "religious neighbors," now we are setting a course in which we have a chance to engage as Jesus would. Fear and/or confusion is the wrong response. Faith in the twenty-first century will move from a focus on religious leaders to a focus on the followers of various faiths. Religious leaders who try to isolate or hold their people back will become increasingly marginalized and disconnected.

In the past four months I've been in Saudi Arabia (from which two hundred thousand students a year are coming to America to be educated); the West Bank (from which immigration to America is the first choice of Palestinians); and a couple of weeks ago in Iraq. Dallas–Fort Worth has a large and growing population of people coming from Iraq. How they are treated here will have direct consequences on how Christians are treated in Iraq. So it's not just about us, our block, and our community; it's about the whole wide world.

Jesus Everywhere

Last Good Friday in Dallas, I was finishing up my message. It was still early in the day, so I thought I should go to the mosque and tell Zia what this day means to me, and invite him to our church. When I asked if I could come over, he said, "Come on, Bob, you're always welcome here." Zia's always made me feel welcome like that.

When I arrived, a man named Farooq took me inside the mosque. We took off our shoes and lined up on the floor. To my left was a friend of Farooq's. He was a businessman, and his son was beside him directly to my left. The little boy wore glasses, and I guessed by his looks that he was probably a child with special needs. So as we began the process of getting up and down and bowing, I began to pray for everyone in that mosque, especially Zia. I prayed for God to use me to love them and reach them.

As we went down on the floor, to my left the boy touched my left hand. This is something no Muslim or someone from the Middle East would do. I turned my head to look at him, and he was grinning ear to ear, his glasses crooked, slobber coming out the corner of his mouth—a beautiful child. I patted his hand and smiled back at him.

In my heart I prayed, "God, you love these people, and I love these people. Let me be your witness, your servant. Give me courage. Your people are here. I am here to be your witness."

Where I am, Jesus is, because he is in me. Jesus was in that mosque as I interceded for those people. Where is Jesus on our streets? Where is Jesus at our schools? Where is Jesus at our jobs? Where is Jesus? He is where we take him. Where are we taking him? He didn't enter us to stay cooped up, but to be bold as love.

NOTES

Chapter One: Boldly Loving All My Neighbors

1. Pew Research Center, "Global Survey of Evangelical Protestant Leaders," June 22, 2011, http://pewresearch.org/pubs/2036/worldwide-evangelical-christian-leaders-poll-lausanne-congress, accessed August 22, 2012.

Chapter Three: Using All My Faith to Get Out on the Edge

1. American Congregations reach out to other Faith Traditions, Sept. 7, 2011. Hartford Institute for Religious Research.

Chapter Five: Requiring All My Truth

1. "The Lausanne Covenant," The Lausanne Movement, www.lausanne.org/en/documents/lausanne-covenant.html (accessed 5 June 2012).

Chapter Seven: Challenging All My Tribe

1. I [Bob Roberts] heard him at a Telos Conference cosponsored by the Aspen Institute in Washington, DC, February 2010.

Chapter Eight: Forgiving with All My Heart

1. Miroslav Volf, *Exclusion & Embrace: A Theological Exploration of Identity, Otherness, and Reconciliation* (Nashville: Abingdon Press, 1996).

ACKNOWLEDGMENTS

I am incredibly grateful for Chris Grant and his partnership since I first began writing in 2005. How can I ever thank Mark Galli for editing my original draft? It was an honor and privilege to work with you. Thank you to Joel Miller, Kristen Parrish, and Janene MacIvor at Thomas Nelson for both publishing and editing.

I am grateful to Northwood Church for taking this journey together with me. You are a boldly loving and courageous church unlike any I know of in the United States. You are always ready for the edge. We keep moving forward, figuring it out as we go, not waiting until it's figured out to go—that's what I love about you. You elders have become my mainstay: Rusty, Chris, Jerry, Ronnie, Gary, and Jim. The staff of Northwood leads by practicing and modeling in truly exceptional ways—especially my administrative assistant Mrs. Carla Felgar.

I'll always be grateful to my wife, Nikki, for walking this trail with me. We have learned so much together and experienced much more life than two people should rightly deserve. I'm proud to be the dad to Jill, who lives this out every day working with the poor and refugees from around the world. I'm honored to have a son, Ben, and a daughter-in-law, Sara, who love those that most would not. Ti and Nghi, you will always be a part of us. You brought Vietnam into our home 24/7.

Bob Buford, Ed Allen, Lylle Wells—thanks for believing in me and speaking into my life over many years.

ABOUT THE AUTHOR

Bob Roberts, Jr., is the founding pastor of Northwood Church in Keller, Texas. He received his master of divinity at Southwestern Baptist Theological Seminary in 1983 and his doctorate in ministry from Fuller in 1996. He has authored *Transformation: How Global Churches Transform Lives and the World*; *Glocalization: How Followers of Jesus Engage a Flat World*; *The Multiplying Church: The New Math for Starting New Churches*; and *Real-Time Connections: Linking Your Job with God's Global Work*. He has written for faith-based publications as well as various diplomatic and global foreign affairs journals. He travels, speaks, and engages in projects all over the world, working with Christians and non-Christians alike, along with various think tanks, state departments, universities, and faith-based organizations. He is married to Nikki, who works with women globally in similar ways. They have two grown children, Ben and Jill.

You can read Bob's blog at
www.glocal.net
and follow him on Twitter
@bobrobertsjr